WHY DOES GOD LET IT HAPPEN?

The Lord's providence is in the smallest details of all, from the first rudiments of our life to its end and beyond to eternity.

—Emanuel Swedenborg, *Secrets of Heaven* §5894

Why Does God Let It Happen?

Bruce Henderson

**SWEDENBORG
FOUNDATION**
West Chester, Pennsylvania

Second printing, 2011. Third printing, 2019.

Library of Congress Cataloging-in-Publication Data

Henderson, Bruce.
       Why does God let it happen? / by Bruce Henderson.
             p. cm.
       Includes bibliographical references.
       ISBN 978-0-87785-332-9 (alk. paper)
1. Providence and government of God--Christianity. 2. Swedenborg, Emanuel, 1688-1772. 3. Theodicy. I. Title.
BT135.H37 2010
231'.5--dc22
           2009049140

Manufactured in the United States of America

Swedenborg Foundation
320 North Church Street
West Chester, PA 19380
www.swedenborg.com

To my wife, Carol,
our children Dan, Glen, and Ellen
and their families—
the blessings of my life

Contents

Introduction

Where was God?

Why did he let this happen?

These are questions as old as human tragedy.

They echoed in the terrorism of the September 11, 2001, attack on the United States.

They haunted the devastation of the tsunami that struck Southeast Asia just after Christmas 2004.

They forever hang over the horror of the Holocaust.

They wrench the souls of people dealing with the loss of children, wives, brothers, parents, and friends.

These questions challenge our faith with every new catastrophe. Why must innocent people suffer? Why can't evil people be thwarted?

Why does God let it happen?

Every calamity revives age-old questions, and the issues are the same whether millions are affected or just one family. Every day we read or hear about some tragedy, perhaps afflicting hundreds or thousands of people, perhaps touching just one child, one family, one circle of loved ones. Each of these tragedies ripples unseen through people's lives, and all are forever changed.

If you are directly impacted, the questions are immediate and insistent: Why me? Why us? Why, God?

Even if you are not personally impacted by another's devastation, you cannot help but wonder: Why would a loving, all-powerful God allow such things to happen? Perhaps even: Is there really a God after all? And if there is, is he really all that loving and all-powerful? Is he really in control? Does he really care about us?

I have been fortunate to have been spared the personal tragedies that inflame these questions. But I have been close enough to people in pain to feel their agony, and throughout a long career in journalism I sensed almost daily the suffering and search for answers when people were suddenly forced to confront these wrenching issues.

Regardless of whether it is individuals, families, communities, or nations, the questions are not new, and the questioners are not alone. These issues have troubled theologians, philosophers, and the common man from the beginning of time. If we believe that God is all-powerful, that he loves us and loves justice, how can he seem to stand by and allow murder, child abuse, cruel diseases, horrible accidents, and untimely death? How can he let innocent people suffer?

These are questions that regularly test our faith. Common to monotheistic religions is a belief in providence—in God's guidance, his omniscience, his plan for our lives. But we are challenged to reconcile innocent faith with harsh reality when we see things happening that just cannot reflect the will of a loving God.

Why didn't God just strike Hitler dead, for instance, before he could inflict such heinous atrocities against millions of innocent people? How can God allow babies to be born blind, mentally impaired, physically handicapped, or afflicted with diseases that will limit their lives on earth? Why does he allow people who seem so undeserving to be born into wealth and privilege, while many good people are pawns to poverty? Why does he permit catastrophes that an all-powerful God should be able to prevent? Why didn't he just reach out his hand to stop those planes on September 11, or those tsunami waves—or the drunken driver who killed a little girl?

Many great writers and thinkers have wrestled with these questions and come away grasping for answers.

C. S. Lewis probed these mysteries in searching books—and found an ultimately transcendent faith. After the death of his wife—so memorably recounted in the film *Shadowlands*—he wrote *A Grief Observed*. Anyone suffering from such agony can identify with his tortured observation, "No one ever told me that grief feels so like fear."[1] That's because grief dares to ask penetrating questions about God and his mercy. The fear is that there may be no satisfying answers—or, as Lewis put it, that he might come to believe "dreadful things" that he did not want to associate with God.[2] Fear denies hope.

One of the most eloquent and compelling attempts in recent years to find answers to these questions is a popular book by Rabbi Harold S. Kushner titled *When Bad Things Happen to Good People*.

Rabbis, priests, and ministers are devoted to nurturing faith in the midst of crises. But when tragedy struck Rabbi Kushner's own home—when his infant son was diagnosed with a disease that would let him live only to age fourteen—the questions became intensely personal and insistent. This wonderful book, which has comforted millions of people, was the result. Its final chapter, especially—"What Good, Then, Is Religion?"—is a must-read for anyone struggling to reconcile a loving God, in control of his universe, with all the chaos and tragedy within it.

But although C. S. Lewis, Rabbi Kushner, and others offer wise and inspiring hope and insights, their answers still are incomplete. After the terrorism of September 11 rocked the world, many religious leaders confessed that they just do not know why God allows such terrible things to happen. They call on faith, but cannot really explain why. It is as though we aren't supposed to know the answers.

Such doubt leaves us confused and hopeless. There has to be a satisfying explanation. We need more than scholarly speculation.

We need something that will validate our faith in God and keep us from doubting or even being angry with him.

Well, there are answers. And there is hope. A thorough, rational explanation of God's enduring providence and his guiding love in everything in life is found in the systematic theology given by God through Emanuel Swedenborg (1688–1772) more than two hundred years ago.

Swedenborg was one of the foremost scientists, philosophers, theologians, and intellects of the eighteenth century—or of any time. He humbly asserted that, during the last twenty-seven years of an amazingly productive life in science and public service, he was given a new revelation from God. In this way, Swedenborg was a prophet like Moses or Matthew. This new revelation unveils the inner meanings of the Bible, describes life after death in vivid detail, and makes clear the spiritual significance of our lives.

Swedenborg wrote twenty-five volumes of closely reasoned doctrine, including a detailed explanation of divine providence—what it is and how it works. His teachings show how God really does lead all aspects of our lives without compromising our freedom; why God allows things against his will for the sake of that freedom; and how he is guiding us and loving us at all times, no matter what the appearance may be to the contrary.

Swedenborg never attempted to start a church or attract a personal following. He said his mission was simply to convey this new revelation as the word of God, which has since been accepted by people all over the world as the basis for a "new Christianity."

Swedenborg's teachings about heaven, hell, and life after death have given comfort and hope to people dealing with the tragedy of death. His revelation has given them a more confident faith about the meaning of their lives on earth and the reality of the life to come.

His teachings about divine providence can do the same for all our nagging questions about why events unfold the way they do. Swedenborg explains that there are absolute spiritual laws that govern God's creation. These "laws of providence" express God's love and guidance in our lives, and his presence never ceases—even when it may seem that he has turned his back or become distant. God can never go against his own laws, which are there to protect our eternal lives, not just our lives on earth.

Many of these teachings will be related to specific examples throughout this book, but four concepts are fundamental:

- God *is* all-powerful and in total control. He never abandons us. But he does allow things that are contrary to his will, for the sake of our freedom, because our freedom is fundamental to his love.

- What God allows but does not will is called "permission" by Swedenborg. Understanding this concept helps to answer the question, "Why?"

- If the tragedy that happens in our lives is the permission, then providence is what happens afterward. It is the way God's love heals and it always leads to good.

- What we see in this natural or material world is limited by space and time. It's temporal. God sees everything in a spiritual context—not only how our lives are affected here and now, but the impact and repercussions to eternity.

God's providence is governed by fixed spiritual laws. It is not arbitrary, but clear and consistent within a transcendent spiritual context. One of these laws, according to Swedenborg, is that God will not permit anything evil that cannot be turned eventually toward good. The potential good that can come from a bad situation isn't obvious in most cases, especially when we are struck by horror, injustice, and sorrow and cannot grasp the overlying spiritual dimension.

Sometimes there's the intimation that a tragedy—the death of a teenager, the loss of thousands in an earthquake—somehow is God's will. We aren't expected to understand it, just to accept it. Swedenborg gives us the comfort that when bad things happen, they are never God's will. He wills only what is good for all of us. And when bad things do happen—because of the freedom he allows—he feels our pain, is present with us (whether we feel it or not), and is always working to bring the best out of the situation.

It is hard to feel such faith when we see only what happens on the material plane of our lives. This makes it challenging to reconcile tragedy and evil with a loving, in-control God. But Swedenborg teaches that from the day we are born, there is a spiritual dimension to our lives that we aren't fully aware of while on earth. This is the life that continues to eternity. God sees everything that happens to us on that spiritual level, free of the limits of time and space in this world, with implications played out to eternity. Swedenborg says that if we could see the working of providence in our lives, it would look like scattered heaps of materials for building a house. Some things connected, some not. Bits of pattern here, chaos there. But God can look at you at any stage of your life and see how all the pieces fit together, like a beautiful home, constantly changing and improving.

Look at the way we see the world disrupted by earthquakes, hurricanes, fires, and other disasters. But the earth always returns to a natural order and a sense of balance. Swedenborg shows how there is spiritual order to God's creation as well, underlying all of the aberrations we witness and wonder about, with those eternal spiritual ramifications that we can never perceive in this life. That doesn't completely answer the question of why. And it doesn't take away the pain. But being given a glimpse into what God sees can help us to understand that even in the midst of the chaos and tragedy we witness, he really does have a plan. He loves us enough to let us be free to make our mistakes, to suffer pain, and even to inflict pain. And his providence is always watching over every aspect of our spiritual lives—which is where life really matters.

Many people, of course, have claimed a special revelation from God, often attracting more skeptics than believers. But people who have read Swedenborg with open, inquiring minds are convinced that he was an extraordinary man, prepared by God for a special mission, and that his insight is unique. Helen Keller called him "an eye among the blind, and an ear among the deaf" and "one of the noblest champions Christianity has ever known."[3] Ralph Waldo Emerson called Swedenborg "a colossal soul who lies vast abroad on his times. He is not to be measured by whole colleges of ordinary scholars."[4] Elizabeth Barrett Browning said simply of Swedenborg's revelation, "It explains much that was incomprehensible."[5]

In the Psalms, David says of God's perfect understanding of man, "Such knowledge is too wonderful for me; it is so high that I cannot attain it."[6] But Swedenborg's teachings give us answers about God's providence and why he allows what seems to contradict his all-loving, all-powerful nature—questions that have always seemed incomprehensible. Now we *can* attain such knowledge. We *are* allowed to know the answers. These teachings convey a sure sense that God's love and leading are always in control and ultimately triumphant. We can put our trust in him, even and especially in the midst of tragedy. And we no longer need to wonder: why does God let it happen?

This is a book that takes the blinders off faith. It is a book, ultimately, about hope and trust.

Why, God?

Truth forever on the scaffold,
Wrong forever on the throne,—
Yet that scaffold sways the future,
And, behind the dim unknown,
Standeth God within the shadows,
Keeping watch above His own.

> —James Russell Lowell, *The Present Crisis*, 1844

No matter how steep the mountain—the Lord is going to climb it with you.

> —Helen Steiner Rice

They say God is everywhere, and yet we always think of Him as somewhat of a recluse.

> —Emily Dickinson

So, WHY DOES God let it happen? Why does he let us live with all the doubts and questions about his love and authority that were raised in the introduction?

Why does he allow the catastrophes we call "acts of God"? Why does he permit war? Suffering? Evil? Yes, why *do* bad things happen to good people? And why do good things happen to bad people?

These questions have their roots in the beginning of time. Why did God put Adam and Eve in the Garden of Eden—then let them be seduced by a serpent and bring sin into the world? Why did Jesus Christ, the human form of God come down to earth, begin his ministry by allowing the devil to tempt him for forty days in the wilderness? Why was there so much trial and testing in the short life of this man of peace? And why did God allow "his only begotten son" to die on the cross?

Swedenborg teaches us that God did not come to earth for a life of peace and ease. He came to conquer the hells so that we could have the promise of heaven.

But still we question. If God truly is in control, why can't he prevent all that's wrong in the world? Why does a loving God sometimes appear angry, punishing, and distant? Why didn't he just create a perfect world where we all could be happy, healthy, and safe—a place where good and innocent people would not suffer?

That is what we understand God's will to be. He wants us to love each other and to live happy, productive lives. He can create anything he wants, and surely he does not want innocent people to suffer. But he lets it happen. Why? We see his miracles in the Old and New Testaments and manifested in his creation, yet we cannot help but wonder at what he apparently chooses not to do.

This can become a real test of faith. We pray for God's protection. We may even feel entitled to it, especially if we assume that we are living good lives. But still God allows what can seem to contradict his protection. Why?

Remember the biblical story where Jacob had stolen his brother Esau's birthright and fled in fear of reprisal? That's when Jacob dreamed of the ladder between heaven and earth, with angels ascending and descending, and the voice of God said to him: "Know that I am with you and will keep you wherever you go."[1] Jacob understood this to mean that his physical life would be protected—and that's the kind of protection we also assume. But what God is really promising is protection for our spiritual well-being, and this is where his providence truly operates.

Those "laws" of divine providence mentioned in the introduction are just that—inflexible laws, not guidelines that can be bent and manipulated on a whim. The whole universe would be unbalanced if God inserted himself between natural cause and effect. But along with these immutable laws is a newly articulated doctrine described by Swedenborg as "permission," which means that God is always providing for our spiritual growth and fulfillment, even if we must experience tragedy and loss in order for that growth to happen.

Swedenborg assures us that while God is allowing us to be free—often blissfully unaware of his spiritual protection—he is still involved in every aspect of our lives, constantly trying to turn bad experiences into good results without compromising our freedom. What is comforting in this revelation is that there is no evil act or tragic accident—horrifying as they may be—that cannot be transformed by God for higher ends. God's will is that all of us can get to heaven, and he does everything he can to lead us there, while still allowing us to choose hell instead.

There is a sort of spiritual common sense to this that many people seem to grasp intuitively without clear explanation or perfect understanding. We may accept, for instance, that there is something called providence and that God does have a plan for our lives, but we accept this more as a matter of faith than with real understanding. It was Swedenborg who finally was able to explain and reconcile providence and "permission." And understanding these basic teachings is what makes faith compatible with reason. It takes away the mystery of a loving God in an "ungodly" world.

Here are the fundamentals:

- God created us as free individuals, and protects that essential freedom enough to allow us to choose between good and evil—ultimately, to choose to spend eternity in heaven or hell. He could have created all of us as angels on earth, but then we would not be free. And if we were not free, we could not be happy—we could not even be human.

- God rules his creation according to consistent laws that apply equally to everyone. He would violate his own nature if he tried to change those laws for anyone or for any reason. He cannot and will not do that.

- God permits only evil that can be turned eventually toward good. Of course, no amount of goodness could bring back the lives lost on September 11, but consider: a few evil people committed that atrocity; millions of people responded with faith, love, and kindness. This is the power that always overcomes the evil.

We've all seen examples of how providence works—blessings coming out of tragedy that we could not have foreseen or anticipated. In the Bible, when Joseph was sold into slavery by his brothers and later confronted them in Egypt, where he had been raised into power by the Pharaoh, he said to them: "Even though you intended to do harm to me, God meant it for good."[2] Even in the depths of the Holocaust, where God may have seemed most remote, Auschwitz survivor Viktor Frankl found hope and meaning in his experience. Out of his experiences in Nazi death camps came his heart-warming and life-changing bestseller *Man's Search for Meaning*, which has had more than seventy printings and been translated into twenty-six languages.

Swedenborg explains why sometimes we can see the workings of divine providence in retrospect—how a "chance" meeting led to a happy marriage, for example, or a tragic accident eventually changed someone's life for the better. Some couples who were devastated to learn they had a Down's syndrome child have come to feel blessed and say, "It was the best thing that could have happened to us." But we never see providence as it is affecting our lives; that would limit our freedom to make our own choices.

What's interesting is that most people—even those who have suffered immensely, like Frankl—usually say they would not change their lives if they had it to do over. It is as though they realize that their life experiences were essential to their personal growth, and that all along they were being led. Probably none of us would choose to endure tragedy or tough times to experience such growth, but we often can see in retrospect that something good has come out of something bad. We certainly saw it in the aftermath of September 11, when the love and compassion of millions of people around the world transcended the horror inflicted by a small number of terrorists. It didn't wipe away the pain, but it did help restore faith that good always eventually triumphs over evil.

It is not in looking back, however, but in coping with what's right in front of us that we are tested. Our faith may be enough to sustain us as long as the questions about God's control of the universe remain abstract. It is when the questions become personal—as they did for Rabbi Kushner and his wife with their son, and as they do every day for people suddenly forced to cope with tragedy—that our faith needs help. Then the questions and doubts about God's fairness and love, his justice and omniscience, become insistent and troubling. Anger can overtake faith if people suddenly feel that living a good life doesn't protect them from evil or misfortune.

In the tiny Pennsylvania town of Montoursville, devastated in the summer of 1996 when the crash of TWA Flight 800 killed a group of students and chaperones traveling to France, a Catholic priest told a grieving congregation never to say or even hint that this was God's will. No doubt the congregation—and a mourning nation—agreed: surely this was not what God wanted to happen. There must have been some bitter thoughts as well: yes, but why couldn't he stop it?

Of course, he could stop earthquakes and cancer and car wrecks. He could have stopped the gunmen who ravaged Columbine High School in 1999 and Virginia Tech in 2007. So why didn't he?

Think about that. Where would you draw the line? It is easy to say stop Hitler, stop the terrorists, stop Hurricane Katrina. But what about the things we can control? We could require governors that keep cars from speeding, ban foods and additives that contribute to weight and health problems, prohibit smoking and alcohol and guns and bombs. But we love our freedom, don't we? We don't want anyone taking it away, even if we might abuse it. Without the freedom to make mistakes that may lead to suffering in our own lives and the lives of others, we would be reduced to automatons.

The same principle works on a spiritual level. If God were to meddle in our lives and change the course of history to preserve our own narrow sense of order and justice, where would he stop? God cannot pick and choose. His laws—and his love—must be absolute and consistent.

As parents, we know that as much as we want to protect our families at all times, we cannot impose such total control that our children are stifled and are not free to develop as individuals. Imagine shadowing your teenager all day and saying, "No, don't do that," or "Yes, that's OK." Yes, you may be loving and protective, but your teenager would have no sense of freedom and would quickly rebel. So we do what we can to protect their safety and give them the guidance they need to make good choices, but we have to let them make mistakes and learn from them. Imagine what would happen if we were prevented from making mistakes—or even from being victimized by them. We wouldn't feel free or in control of our own lives, either.

We don't stop our children from learning to drive when they are of age. We teach and preach safety, and we worry when they are on the road. But if an accident happens, we don't blame parents who have been loving and responsible. We know how they worry, and how they grieve over tragedies involving their children. But we know that part of loving our children is letting them be free, within reasonable limits, comforting them when accidents happen, and helping them learn the right lessons.

We need to remember that we are all God's children and that his love for each of us is more intense, consuming, and compassionate than our love for our own children. He gives us freedom, too—allows us to do what he would not will for us—with all the love and guidance anyone could want. He grieves for all of us when we make bad choices or are victims of misfortune.

He does not turn his back, as it may seem. He is always there, with his providence, creating the potential for a good outcome. The good may be in our spiritual lives, after passing from this world, and it may not be readily apparent on this natural level of life. But it is on that unseen spiritual plane where the effects of all events reflect his will and last forever. That ultimately is what his providence is all about—allowing us to make free choices, even if they aren't the best choices or the right choices in his eyes, while always striving to lift us up to heaven and providing the means to do so.

Throughout history, the image of God has not always been of an all-loving figure who is looking out for our best interests. In the Old Testament, God sometimes is portrayed as angry and vengeful. Because of that, the notion has arisen that disasters and diseases may be God's way of punishing us for sin. So when people get sick or suffer, they may think they somehow deserve it. But in the New Testament, when a man who was born blind was brought before Jesus, his disciples asked: "Master, who sinned, this man or his parents, that he was born blind?" And Jesus answered, "Neither this man nor his parents sinned; he was born blind so that God's works might be revealed in him."[3]

So where, then, do evil and misfortune come from, if not from God? Swedenborg asserts that anything not of God's will has its origin in hell. Anything from hell, of course, is not what God wants for us, but he allows hell and its influence in our lives for the sake of our freedom. He wants all of us to choose his way and heaven, but loves us enough to give us the choice.

If we are to be truly free, however, to make the choice between heaven and hell, we need to know more about them. Swedenborg teaches that on earth we are in constant equilibrium between heaven and hell, subject to influences from each. We certainly glimpse aspects of heaven and hell in our everyday lives, from moments of blissful love, peace, and fulfillment to flashes of anger, hatred, and frustration. We are constantly making choices and can also be affected by other people's choices, even harmed by them.

Even if we don't want to be selfish, cruel, lazy, angry, or lustful, what would life be like if we were not free to make such choices—and learn from them? Imagine if this was a perfect world where nothing bad could ever happen: Wouldn't we feel like puppets, with no freedom to act on our own? We not only would not feel free, we would not feel responsible or challenged to make things better. This is what God's love is all about: letting us be free, but using his providence to help us overcome whatever befalls us, even when we are unaware of that influence in this life.

Swedenborg assures us that God "never curses anyone, is never angry at anyone, never leads anyone into crisis. He does not even punish us, let alone curse us. It is the Devil's crew that does such things. Nothing of the sort could ever come from the fountain of mercy, peace, and goodness."[4]

God operates entirely from love. He created us so that he can share his love with us. But he cannot—will not—force us to return his love, because that would violate our freedom. This is the ultimate in unconditional love. We are always free to accept his love, to reject it, or to be indifferent to it. And our choices may fluctuate until we are clearly ready to choose one way or the other—the cumulative choice that ultimately leads each of us to the eternal "home" we have chosen, in heaven or hell.

You might think God would compel us to love him and to live justly and peacefully with each other. But his love is so great that he allows us to choose, even if it grieves him when we choose against him. This permission to do evil—for the sake of our freedom—is what gives rise to the tragedies and injustice that afflict our world and victimize innocents. But his love is unceasing and always for good purposes.

Instead of wondering why God would allow bad things to happen to good people, we should be considering why *we* allow so many bad things to happen to each other. Wars and crime, corruption and pollution, emotional and physical abuse, and diseases and accidents are products of our own actions and choices. So let's ask ourselves: Why do people corrupt themselves and pollute our atmosphere, causing disease to others? Why are they cruel and violent to others, whether in global wars or personal crime? Why do they destroy their own marriages and families, betray friends, and inflict pain on those they love? Just as we might wish that God had struck Hitler dead before he could inflict his evil on the world, we might wish that God could eliminate all our sins and faults so that no one need suffer because of them. But that would not be leaving anyone in freedom. That would not really be loving us.

We can wonder, with Rabbi Kushner, why "the wrong people" get sick or hurt, or die young. We can agonize with him over the "deep, aching sense of unfairness" over his son's terminal disease. As people who are trying to do what is right in God's sight—living a religiously committed life—we would be tempted to ask the same question: If God truly is loving and fair, "How could he do this to me?" And not only how could he do this to "good parents," but how could he do this to an innocent, three-year-old child?

This is where people struggle with their faith, because they have not had complete answers. Throughout history, religious faith has tended to promote guilt, as though somehow whatever happens must be a person's own fault. Swedenborg makes it possible, finally, to understand that what does not seem fair to our eyes can all fit beautifully and meaningfully into the spiritual continuum of God's sight, where he alone can see where his providence leads.

Rabbi Kushner has articulated the questions so well for so many people. He understands that God does not cause the bad things that happen to us, and that God does not sit on his throne, determining which of us will suffer misfortunes and which will be spared. But he does stand always ready to help, comfort, and lead. "The God I believe in," Kushner wrote, "does not send us the problem; he gives us the strength to cope with the problem."[5]

Kushner also is right in observing—as did Frankl in the midst of the Holocaust—that every individual, no matter how grievous the circumstances or unfortunate a childhood, still is free to make choices about his or her life. When we are tempted to ask where God was in the horror of the Holocaust, Kushner replies that he *was* there—loving the victims and agonizing with them, but without controlling man's choosing between good and evil. That is man's choice, man's freedom, the one thing a loving God will not take away. And Kushner came to see, through his and his wife's own struggle, that the question we need to focus on is not where tragedy comes from, but where it leads. It can lead from despair to hope, from hell to heaven. This is what God's providence ultimately is all about.

Two poignant stories that probe the mysteries of God's love, power and perfection—and the circumstances that seem to contradict them—can help us grapple with the kinds of questions that gnawed at Kushner and Frankl. One is the biblical account of Job, who was the object of a contest between God and Satan. The other is a classic short novel by Thornton Wilder, *The Bridge of San Luis Rey*. Both are cited by Rabbi Kushner in his own search for answers. Both resonate with our lives and echo our fears and doubts. And both can be understood more clearly in light of the revelation given through Swedenborg, especially in his teachings about how providence works and how "permission" is part of God's providence. Swedenborg also explains the story of Job from a spiritual perspective, describing it as an allegory about the desolation of the spirit and its ultimate triumph.

Job was a man who was "blameless and upright, one who feared God and turned away from evil."[6] He had been blessed with wealth and a large family. But his character was attacked by Satan. He lost his family and his property. And he became the ultimate example of bad things happening to a good person.

Job was philosophical about being tested and was unyielding in his faith, even when Satan afflicted his body with boils. But eventually he cursed his birth and longed for death. He came to the question that has troubled many sincere believers who see pain and suffering all around them: "If I sin, what do I do to you, you watcher of humanity? Why have you made me your target? Why have I become a burden to you? Why do you not pardon my transgression and take away my iniquity?"[7]

Job is the enduring symbol of someone who was not apparently a sinner, who tried to live a good, decent life, who loved God—and still was a victim of cruel misfortune. It seems as though God was inflicting the punishment, or at least was indifferent to it. So why Job? Why this good man? It doesn't seem fair.

But none of the horrors suffered by Job were inflicted by God. Yes, they were permitted by God. And Job and his friends assumed that whatever God permits, he must cause. Even Jesus's own disciples did the same when confronted with the blind man. However, as we see in Swedenborg's teachings about providence, God does not permit anything that cannot be turned to good—even if we aren't always aware of the transcendent spiritual context that God sees and we do not. And sure enough, "The Lord restored the fortunes of Job . . . and the Lord gave Job twice as much as he had before."[8] Not only was he blessed materially but, as so often happens when any of us endure hard times, he had a far deeper understanding and appreciation of his life.

That is something we also see with Frankl, a man who suffered just as unfairly and horrifically as Job did. But after his liberation from Auschwitz, Frankl was walking in a meadow and suddenly felt overcome, sinking to his knees. "I called to the

Lord from my narrow prison," he wrote, "and he answered me in the freedom of space. In that hour, my new life started."[9]

What Frankl found was that when all life's familiar goals are snatched away, "the last of human freedoms [is] to choose one's attitude"—and he chose faith, optimism, and hope.[10] Most of us would be more inclined to doubt, denial, and despair. Frankl's attitude, the one thing he still was free to control, is what allowed him to rise above Auschwitz and not be completely victimized by the experience.

But what about when God seems almost to choose the victims of accidents, tragedies, and disease—or, at least, does not choose to spare them?

The Bridge of San Luis Rey was Thornton Wilder's attempt to make sense of the seeming randomness of victims. Is it all just bad luck? Is it really God's will? Is he somehow powerless in such situations? Are we all predestined to our fate? Is there a divine plan to each and every life, or is it all just random acts and consequences?

Wilder builds his story around five ordinary people who fall to their deaths in 1714 when a rope bridge—"the finest bridge in Peru"—breaks and sends them plunging into a gorge. So why these five, and not those who crossed just before or those who were to follow?

Brother Juniper, who witnesses the accident, is left to try to reconcile this tragedy with the nature of God. Wilder writes that as those who had just crossed the bridge, or were about to, marveled at their fortune, "It was another thought that visited Brother Juniper: 'Why did this happen to *those* five?' If there were any plan in the universe at all, if there were any pattern in a human life, surely it could be discovered mysteriously latent in those lives so suddenly cut off. Either we live by accident and die by accident, or we live by a plan and die by a plan."[11]

So Brother Juniper set about trying to discover some hidden explanation that would make sense of it all. He investigated

their lives and even came up with a rating of each victim's goodness, piety, and usefulness. He speculated that since each had
just resolved some problem and was ready to enter a new phase
of life, maybe there is "a right time" to die. And he concluded,
with a mix of frustration and wisdom: "Soon we shall die and all
memory of those five will have left the earth, and we ourselves
shall be loved for a while and forgotten. But the love will have
been enough; all those impulses of love return to the love that
made them. Even memory is not necessary for love. There is a
land of the living and a land of the dead and the bridge is love,
the only survival, the only meaning."[12]

Rabbi Kushner found Wilder's speculation interesting but
"ultimately unsatisfying." If we substitute hundreds of victims of
an airplane crash, he wrote, "it strains the imagination to claim
that every single one of them had just passed a point of resolu-
tion in his life."[13] In fact, we often learn that they were in the
midst of important work, had plans for the future, or left young
families. Kushner finds a better explanation in a book Wilder
wrote forty years later, *The Eighth Day*, which is about a good
and decent man whose life is ruined by bad luck. In this book,
Wilder offers the image of a tapestry that shows an inspiring
work of art on one side but a tangle of threads and knots on the
other.

"Wilder offers this as an explanation," Kushner writes, "of
why good people have to suffer in this life. God has a pattern
into which all of our lives fit. His pattern requires that some lives
be twisted, knotted, or cut short, while others extend to impres-
sive lengths, not because one thread is more deserving than
another, but simply because the pattern requires it. Looked at
from underneath, from our vantage point in life, God's pattern
of reward and punishment seems arbitrary and without design,
like the underside of a tapestry. But looked at from outside this
life, from God's vantage point, every twist and knot is seen to
have its place in a great design that adds up to a work of art."[14]

We do not live in a heaven on earth, but in a proving ground where our souls are tested, where we have choices, and where we may even be victimized unfairly, but where our spiritual lives and freedom are always protected.

The horror of experiences like Frankl's may help us to reflect that hardship and challenges often are what form our character, like the priceless pearl molded through years of irritation in the oyster.

In the Sermon on the Mount, where Jesus teaches that we should not only love our neighbor but love our enemies, we read: "For he makes his sun to rise on the evil and on the good, and sends rain on the righteous and the unrighteous."[15] God loves everyone and abandons no one, no matter what our personal circumstances or whether we believe in him.

We may rail at the apparent injustice of a beloved, aging parent suffering in the throes of death or Alzheimer's, or a bright young person seemingly taken indiscriminately on the very brink of life—as though we might choose much more wisely.

But after all the rantings of Job and his friends, God answered them "out of the whirlwind" and said: "Who is this that darkens counsel by words without knowledge? . . . Where were you when I laid the foundations of the earth? Tell me, if you have understanding."[16]

"If you have understanding." It is easy to succumb to the illusion of wisdom, to the arrogance that we know better. A college professor once posed this scenario to a class: "A certain man has syphilis. His wife has tuberculosis. Of their four children, one has died and the other three suffer from an incurable illness that is considered terminal. The mother is pregnant. What should she do?" Most of the students didn't hesitate to say she should have an abortion. "Well," said the professor, "you just killed Beethoven."[17]

Yes, we who set the world aflame with wars, abandon whole nations of people to disease and starvation, let our culture slide toward depravity and increasingly cannot keep marriages and families together, we dare to think we could better plan and run the world.

Against our arrogance and despair, our bewilderment and our search for answers, Swedenborg offers explanation, clarity, and hope.

Everything that we see as fate, coincidence, serendipity, good fortune, or bad luck falls under God's providence. If we could see what God sees, we would understand that everything that happens to us—good and bad—is an example of how he is always with us, and of the loving order that permeates everything of his creation.

This is the ultimate prescription for peace. As Swedenborg wrote, "Peace holds within itself trust in the Lord, the trust that he governs all things and provides all things, and that he leads toward an end that is good."[18]

Many of us have an almost instinctive feel for God's guidance and providence in our lives. It is why a father whose daughter and son-in-law died while on a dream trip to Paris in the tragic crash of that TWA Flight 800 in 1996 was able to say with simple faith and heartfelt confidence: "We wake up to a sunrise, but they wake up to a sunrise many times more glorious. We know where they are and we will see them again."[19]

Some people never get beyond the pain and doubt of "Why, God?" But many people come to share the abiding faith of this grieving father. For all of us, finally, there are answers—answers that make sense and bring peace.

Where Is God? In His Providence

God does not play dice.

—Albert Einstein

We failed, but in the good providence of God apparent failure often proves a blessing.

—Robert E. Lee

Trials are medicines which our gracious and wise Physician prescribes because we need them; and he proportions the frequency and weight of them to what the case requires. Let us trust his skill and thank him for his prescription.

—Isaac Newton

THE TSUNAMI THAT swept away whole villages and took the lives of more than 160,000 adults and children in Southeast Asia on a sunny, peaceful day after Christmas in 2004 is yet another tragic setting for the agonizing cry: Where was God? Why did he let this happen? Why?

In the chaos of shattered lives, devastated families, and abject need, these are troubling questions defying easy answers.

The tsunami of 2004 was an eerie echo of an equally cataclysmic earthquake and tsunami 250 years ago in Portugal. That disaster was closely followed by another apparent test of God's love and power—the first truly global war, which forever changed the world. And in the chain of consequences resulting from such tragic events, we begin to see the healing, guiding hand of his providence—the beginning of an answer to the question: why?

The year was 1755, a watershed time in human history, where hard questions and the glimmer of answers began to come into focus.

Repercussions from the relatively obscure Seven Years' War—also known as the French and Indian War—spread from America to Europe, Africa, and Asia, and the world was forever changed. The Treaty of Paris that ended the war in 1763 laid the foundation for the British Empire, provided the springboard for the Industrial Revolution, and sowed the seeds for the American Revolution.

The conquest of Canada and the removal of the French threat made the American colonies much less dependent on Britain for protection. And when the British tried to tax the colonies to help pay the massive costs of the war, that sparked the flame for the American Revolution. Despite the eventual loss of the American colonies, conquests in Africa and the Indian subcontinent in the Seven Years' War, plus a vast increase in the British merchant fleet, helped establish a British Empire upon which "the sun never set." Control of Africa and India also released a flow of gold into Britain. Restless innovators in Britain and the New World were ready to unleash new ideas and inventions to ease labor and increase productivity, and this new wealth unleashed the Industrial Revolution.

It was just a few months after the Seven Years' War began and set these profound changes in motion that a devastating earthquake struck Lisbon on November 1, 1755. Experts estimate that it would have registered 8.5 to 9 on the Richter scale, making it one of the most powerful earthquakes of all time. More than sixty thousand people perished—first from the earthquake itself, then from a massive tsunami about an hour later that also sent deadly tidal waves along the coasts of Iberia and North Africa. The tremors were so strong, they set church bells ringing in distant parts of Europe.

Those tolling bells were ominously significant because the quake struck Lisbon at 9:30 a.m. on All Saints' Day, one of the most important religious celebrations in the Christian world, at a time when the churches were filled. Many worshippers died in their pews. It's no wonder people began speculating on the disaster as an act of God's vengeance or judgment.

There could not have been a more auspicious part of the world for this disaster. Lisbon was known as the Queen of Cities—capital of Portugal, center of a colonial empire, and a gloried stronghold of the Catholic Church, perhaps even more so at that time than Rome. Protestant preachers were quick to advance the notion that this catastrophe was a judgment on the Catholic Church.

The shock waves were significant, felt throughout commerce, government, and the Christian world, so questions about God's vengeance—or his absence—were inevitable.

The impact on religion and philosophy, and on personal faith, was transforming. Traditional Christianity prior to the earthquake was described as sublime, with people generally "content in God," unquestioning in their beliefs, and submissive to authority. The enormity of this tragedy quickly became a catalyst by challenging the popular notion that all things happen for a reason in this "best of all possible worlds."

French philosopher and writer François-Marie Arounet (1694–1778), better known under his pen name, Voltaire, led the new wave of cynicism and scorn, first with his *Poème sur le désastre de Lisbonne* (*Poem on the Disaster at Lisbon*), then with his withering satirical novel *Candide*. Voltaire savagely mocked the silly optimists who found comfort in God and his protection. This was his own bitter, dismissive response to the question, where was God?

To Voltaire it was obvious that God was not there—certainly not a God who was loving and all-powerful. Such a God surely would not have allowed such devastation and suffering. Such doubt and cynicism are inevitable without understanding how providence and permission work.

But whether or not people made the connection, good things were happening as a result of the Lisbon tragedy. Strict orthodoxy began giving way to open minds and freedom of speech. New ideas were no longer scorned or suppressed but welcomed. There was an evangelical revival in England and missionary efforts to translate the Bible and spread it throughout the British Empire, which later would touch all corners of the world.

How much did all of this relate to an apparently random earthquake and a relatively minor war? Was it all just coincidence—the natural progression of cause and effect—or was there perhaps a divine "plan" at work to bring good results out of a devastating event? People can choose to see the possibilities either way. But an informed faith about the workings of divine providence, the understanding that God does permit what he does not will for the sake of our freedom, begins to answer the nagging questions of why things happen the way they do.

Consider other examples, from the Bible and from history, that may raise doubts about God's control in some cases, but tend to confirm the operation of his providence in others.

From the beginning of the Bible (Adam and Eve being seduced by the serpent in the Garden of Eden) to the end (the crucifixion of God's "only begotten Son"), people have wondered why God would allow such assaults on his power. Others have come to see these tests as the ultimate examples of permission and providence, which forever provide for our freedom and salvation.

History also is replete with tantalizing examples. England's King Henry VIII in the early 1500s, for example, was a self-absorbed madman, executing wives in pursuit of a male heir and breaking with the Catholic Church to assert his power and indulge his desires. But what he set in motion, the establishment of the Protestant movement, inadvertently established the foundation for religious freedom all over Europe, which carried over to America.

In 1588, King Phillip II of Spain sent his army aboard the Spanish Armada to invade and conquer Britain. An unusual storm—which came to be known as the "Protestant wind"—helped to destroy the Spanish fleet and spare Britain. The British, in thanks for what they saw as divine intervention, commissioned a commemorative medal inscribed: "He blew with His winds, and they were scattered." Swedenborg, of course, would not agree that it was "divine intervention" and that God "blew his winds." The "natural disaster" for the Spanish was not God's will, but his providence led to what history—and certainly the British—generally see as a good end.

Just as recently as the terrorist attacks of 2001, we saw blatant evil met by an outpouring of kindness and good will, so much so that September 11 anniversaries have become a day for good deeds all over the United States. Such examples tend to confirm a basic tenet of divine providence: that God will not permit anything that cannot be turned toward good and that he is always doing all he can to lead us to heaven.

Albert Einstein (1879–1955), one of the greatest minds to probe the mysteries of the universe, said simply, "God does not play dice." He was convinced there were immutable laws and a form of order at play, not chaos and coincidence. Explaining why he was not an atheist, he wrote: "We are in the position of a little child entering a huge library filled with books in many different languages. The child knows someone must have written those books. It does not know how. It does not understand the languages in which they were written. The child dimly suspects a mysterious order in the arrangement of the books but doesn't know what it is." [1]

Einstein assumed that eventually we would discover those laws. What he didn't know is that they had been "discovered"—actually, revealed to Emanuel Swedenborg—and so made available to all of us to explain that "acts of God" are not tragedies, but rather the unseen manifestations of how he always leads us from bad events to good outcomes.

But if God "does not play dice"—does not gamble with our lives or intervene to manipulate events—and really is in ultimate control, how exactly does he operate? How does his providence work?

The first thing to understand is that in all of creation, in everything that affects your life and the lives of others, God operates according to absolute laws. They are like the laws of nature. Imagine the chaos if gravity worked in some situations but not in others; if results varied when chemicals were combined, depending on who was doing the mixing. These laws do not restrict our freedom but provide for it. It is the same with providence.

It may seem contradictory that an all-powerful God is constrained by laws. It may seem cruel and unloving that exceptions aren't made to prevent bad things from happening to good, innocent, faithful people. What we call the laws of nature are precise, orderly, and predictable. We know when the sun will rise and set, the rhythm of the tides, the sequence of the seasons. We see how nature always returns to balance after a forest fire. What we so glibly call "acts of God," such as earthquakes, hurricanes, and floods, are really acts of nature. The acts of God are in the healing. And so it is in our own lives.

God is consistent in the way he operates because he has to be. Acting against the laws of his providence would be to defy his divine essence—who he is. He just would not be God if he was constantly compromising and adjusting his laws.

So what are these laws?

🙡 *The first law* is that God allows evil to exist for the sake of our freedom. We must be in a state of equilibrium—between good and evil, heaven and hell—to be free to choose the quality of our lives. Without that freedom, we would not feel life to be our own.

🙡 *The second law* is that we must be free to act from our own will, as long as we are making rational choices. Swedenborg says that people cannot be reformed if they are in states of fear, disease, insanity, or ignorance, when they aren't able to make informed, rational decisions. But as long as we are of sound mind and body, we must be free to choose—even if what we choose is not what God would want for us.

❧ *The third law* is that we should not be compelled to believe in God, in his providence, or in anything, because compulsion takes away freedom. Puppets and robots don't have freedom. Wars have been fought to suppress freedom or to win it, including the freedom to believe as we choose and live accordingly. No one wants to be coerced. God wants for us to make good choices, but he will not—cannot—force us to do so. God's will is that each and every one of us gets to heaven by making good choices, by actually choosing heaven in the way we lead our lives. But he will leave people free to reject him, to embrace evil and to choose hell.

❧ *The fourth law* is that for us to be truly free, we must be able to see and recognize evil in order to reject it. This is the challenge of freedom. Our culture is a smorgasbord of good and bad choices. We know what it's like to be tempted, but we also know what the healthy choices are. And we know what it is to live with the consequences of good and bad choices.

❧ *The fifth law* is that the operation of divine providence should never be evident to us, but that we should always know that it is working in our lives. Imagine if you could know how God was leading you. You would feel your freedom was threatened and probably would want to rebel, especially if God was trying to lead you out of a destructive habit while you were still enjoying it and not ready to give it up. We may get glimpses of providence at work when we look back over a chain of events, but not while it's happening.[2]

We often wish we could know the future, for good and bad reasons. But knowing what will happen would take away our freedom, especially if the outcome was something we didn't want at the time. Knowing the future would destroy our freedom to choose, and it would deprive us of something essential to our growth: hope.

Swedenborg teaches that longing to know the future really has its origins in evil, however innocent it may seem. Those who trust in the Lord's guidance in their lives have no desire to know what's going to happen beforehand. As Jesus said to his disciples: "Do not keep striving for what you are to eat and what you are to drink, and do not keep worrying. For it is the nations of the world that strive after all these things, and your Father knows that you need them. Instead, strive for his kingdom, and these things will be given to you as well." [3]

Swedenborg says a man lost in a forest is likely to give himself the credit if he finds his way out. Or maybe he'll say he was just lucky. But all the time, providence was standing in a tower, seeing everything and secretly leading him to safety.

This is what providence does. It is God's continuous process with each one of us to lead us to salvation and to heaven, step by step, through every phase of our lives—but always leaving us free to choose against what God wills for us. The same laws of providence and permission are operating whatever our choices and experiences may be. The outcome depends on whether we are cooperating with God or rejecting him. But his love never stops flowing, like the sun shining and rain falling equally on the roses and the weeds. We all get the same measure; it's up to us how we use it.

The basic concept of providence—of a divine plan somehow operating in our lives and everything happening for a reason—makes sense to many people, even if they don't understand exactly how it works. One reason why it can be difficult to comprehend is because we are limited by space and time. God isn't. He sees our lives in the spiritual context of eternity. As we've noted, we may glimpse some reason for why things happen, but cannot begin to see it all play out the way God does.

The ultimate question is not where tragedy comes from—certainly not from God—but where it leads. God is always leading us toward good outcomes, toward heaven, if we will just follow him.

But it takes more than blindly following God and trusting in his guidance to get us to that "good end." God does not want us living passively with our arms at our sides, just letting life happen, believing he will save us without our effort. He wants us to be making good, active choices and living as best we can to cooperate with his plan.

If we are really to be led by providence, we are commanded to be good stewards of the talents and abilities that have been given to us by being useful and being accountable. Jesus uses the parable of the talents[4] to illustrate that the servants who put their "talents" (a sum of money) to use were rewarded, while the servant who was fearful and buried his talents was rebuked for wasting his opportunity and responsibility.

By living good and useful lives, obeying and living God's commandments, we place ourselves in the stream of his providence. When we cooperate with God in our actions—by being kind and helpful to others, for instance, instead of criticizing and gossiping—we allow his plan of leading us to good to work in our lives.

The more we understand the "doctrine of permissions"—why God allows what he does not will for the sake of our freedom and salvation—the stronger our trust in his providence will be. His love and his mercy are infinite. Our knowledge is always imperfect. How little we know, really, of the challenges we must face, or how much tragedy and testing we must endure, to provide just the right mix of providence and permission that God knows is necessary for our salvation. Through any pain and suffering that afflicts our lives, how comforting it is to know that God is always looking toward our ultimate happiness in heaven where he "will wipe every tear from their eyes. Death will be no more; mourning and crying and pain will be no more, for the first things have passed away."[5]

Deliver Us from Evil

The belief in a supernatural source of evil is not necessary; men alone are quite capable of every wickedness.

—Joseph Conrad, *Under Western Eyes*

Evil is unspectacular and always human, and shares our bed and eats at our own table.

—W. H. Auden

Freud's great courage led him to look honestly at evil in men's nature. He persisted in his research to the bottom of the jar, and there he found hope. He discerned that love is stronger than hate and that for all its care of malignancy the nature of men can be transformed through the nature and dispersion of love. In this way, the destructiveness can be transcended.

—Dr. Karl Menninger

"Deliver us from evil." The words echo from the prayer Jesus Christ taught in his Sermon on the Mount, words still invoked every day by Christians the world over.

These words acknowledge that evil exists in the world, that we are all susceptible to it, and that only God can truly deliver us—save us—from its power.

But why does God allow evil in the world? And how are we to reconcile a God we like to think of as loving and all-powerful with what is contrary to his love, his truth, and all that he wants for us?

Evil is a strong word. We tend to reserve it for tyrants, abusers, murderers—the worst criminals and heartless souls whose actions are clearly despicable. We all do bad things from time to time. We can be selfish and unkind, but we don't like to think of ourselves as "evil."

However, "evil" is used throughout the Bible to describe any of our wayward leanings that turn us away from God.

We might forgive the children of Israel for "making mistakes" during their forty years of trial and suffering in the wilderness. But the Bible says: "[They] had done evil in the sight of the Lord."[1]

We may see people as a mix of good and bad intentions. The Bible says: "The inclination of the human heart is evil from youth."[2]

The Bible doesn't tell us not to make bad choices. It says: "Remove the evil of your doings from before my eyes; cease to do evil, learn to do good."[3]

Obviously, there are many degrees of what may be lumped under "evil," from white lies to the most heinous crimes. Swedenborg says the all-encompassing definition of evil in the biblical context is simply the act of turning away from God, or doing anything that opposes the happiness he wants for us. It is easy to see the horror of Hitler, for example, as abject evil. He deliberately and defiantly turned his back on anything and everything of God. Other ways of turning our backs can be much more subtle: a bad mood, a lapse of judgment, or flashes of anger, spite, and frustration. In its broadest terms, evil doesn't apply just to the worst people among us, but at some times to all of us. We all see glimpses of hell in our lives when we turn our backs on God, if just for a few moments of selfishness or hatefulness. And we all know feelings of heaven when we turn toward God, even if unconsciously, by being kind, helping others, or just taking the time to appreciate the glories of nature. That's what our freedom—ultimately, the freedom to choose heaven or hell throughout our lives—is all about.

Swedenborg teaches us that we are all born to go to heaven, and we have a lot of good traits learned from our parents, plus all the power of God and heaven, to help us get there. But ever since the serpent seduced Adam and Eve in the Garden of Eden to eat of the forbidden Tree of the Knowledge of Good and Evil—the "original sin"—all of us also have what Swedenborg calls "hereditary evils." These are not actual evils or sins within us, but inclinations or tendencies to turn away from God. We may feel those tugs throughout our lives. But we don't really "own" a sin unless we consciously make it our own by choosing it and delighting in it.

The battle of good versus evil has been an enduring theme throughout history, in art, literature, and culture, from David and Goliath to Luke Skywalker and Darth Vader. One of the classic portrayals of this struggle was Fyodor Dostoevsky's novel *Crime and Punishment*. It is the story of Raskolnikov, who proudly conceives a "perfect crime"—the murder of a spiteful pawnbroker. It's for the common good, he tells himself. The world would be better off without this miserable person. It was easy to give himself permission to transcend the law, just as we may glibly rationalize our own indulgences. But he finds himself tormented by guilt and conscience.

The story becomes a morality tale as Raskolnikov is torn between his evil nature and what he knows to be right. He comes to discover the workings of providence, although he does not know it as such, when he sees something good coming from his evil, but not by his own power. And he learns the lesson we all need to understand. When we feel supremely self-confident, trusting solely in ourselves and the world, we fight alone, we have no hope, and we are doomed to frustration and unhappiness. But when we trust in God and allow him to lead, we are never alone. Only then can we achieve success and find happiness.

To that end, Swedenborg says, it is also important to know that evil does not originate with us. We may all have a dark side at times, experiencing troubling thoughts and doing things we know are wrong or come to regret. But however much it may seem that we are alone with our sometimes good/sometimes bad nature, evil actually comes from outside of us, not inside. All evil originates in hell and influences us from there.

The world may seem to be overflowing with evil. Look at our wayward culture: pervasive pornography on the Internet, rampant crime and abuse, cruel persecution of whole groups of people, and the horror of terrorism. But the world is not innately evil. Neither is any one of us evil unless we choose of our own free will to act on evil inclinations. Evil is always a perversion by human beings of what God created as a good thing.

Love of self and love of the world are not inherently evil. Looking out for ourselves and our families is the responsible thing to do, as long as we don't put ourselves above God and everyone else, or love the physical things of this world more than the spiritual qualities of heaven.

Philosopher Jean-Jacques Rousseau (1712–1778) said, "God makes all things good; man meddles with them and they become evil."[4] Swedenborg would add: Yes, it is man, not God, who chooses evil; but man can just as easily choose good. In fact, we are either turning toward God or away from him throughout every moment of our lives. What makes the difference is that through the pattern of our lives, we ultimately choose one way over the other—either heaven or hell. But there is a lot of turning back and forth in the process.

That's why no one should feel guilty or set apart just because they do bad things at times, or entertain bad thoughts. We may feel guilty about such lapses only if we no longer see them as bad, have no desire to shun them, and have no pangs of conscience. God always forgives if we are sincere in fighting against whatever evils may tempt us.

The ultimate promise in the way God governs is that no matter what evil is inflicted on the world, he is always working to bend it toward good. Unfortunately, innocent people do suffer and grieve because of what we do to each other, but in the timelessness of his spiritual kingdom, where we all will live forever, is that eternal promise of God wiping away our tears, with no more sorrow, crying, or pain.[5]

In times of tragedy, that assurance of "no more pain" may not be easy to accept. But think how much worse it would be if God was not there constantly working to offset sorrow with hope.

It comes down to this: Either there is a loving God who permits what he does not will for the sake of our freedom, but keeps leading us toward heaven, or God isn't all that loving and powerful after all—and maybe doesn't even exist. Swedenborg assures us over and over that God's love and mercy are always there through all the trials of life, and are ultimately triumphant.

Swedenborg also explains clearly that just as the good flowing in from God and heaven needs to be a part of our lives, we need to know and experience evil also. Wouldn't it be nice if we didn't have to worry about bad people or bad things happening to us? But for the sake of our freedom and ultimate salvation, we need to be in equilibrium in this life. Only by knowing both good and evil are we able to choose to reject evil and then be cleansed of it through a life of regeneration, which in Swedenborgian terms means repenting from bad things we've done and following God rather than our own inclinations. When we do that, heaven will protect us forever from anything evil.

We've all seen cartoons of a man with the devil on one shoulder and an angel on the other, competing for his attention and trying to get him to go one way or the other. That's not so far-fetched. Swedenborg says we are constantly in the company of good and evil spirits from the spiritual world. We aren't aware of them, and they don't know that they are with us specifically. They aren't watching our lives and spying on what we are doing. But just as people on this earth have what we call a "presence"—something about their character that influences our good or bad instincts—the spheres of good and evil spirits are said to be with us, almost like that cartoon angel and devil. God keeps us from being overwhelmed by one or the other so that we are always free to choose. We are choosing all the time whose company we want to keep, whether we want the angels or the devils in our lives. Think about that: we aren't conscious of this influence from heaven and hell, but it is a part of us—every day, every moment—as we pick our way along our journey.

One reason why God allows us to experience the consequences of bad choices is to provide an incentive to change our lives for the better, to grow spiritually through regeneration.

Another reason is so that we can experience what life looks like when we don't follow God and his commandments. Hopefully, this helps us to choose a better path.

Whatever path we are on, God never stops working for us and with us. But we have to work with him also. Remember what Jesus said to Nicodemus: "Very truly, I tell you, no one can see the kingdom of God without being born from above."[6] And when Nicodemus asked how an old man could be born again, Jesus said he must be "born of water and Spirit."[7] According to Swedenborg, this describes a process of reformation and regeneration—consciously choosing against evil and for good through self-examination, reflection, and repentance or atonement. That practice of self-improvement can last a lifetime and even continue after death.

Freedom is fundamental to this process. But there are two kinds of freedom, one hellish and one heavenly. Heavenly freedom is exercising freedom responsibly by thinking and doing what's right in the eyes of God and what is best for everyone. If we are thinking bad thoughts and acting on them—just doing what we want and not caring about others, even if they might be hurt or threatened—that is freedom, too, but it's a hellish kind of freedom.

What's the difference? They both feel free, but they are opposites, and only one can be true freedom. Think about driving safely and obeying the rules versus ignoring stop signs or driving on the wrong side of the road. We have the freedom to choose either of those behaviors, but the impulses come from very different places, with different results. Jesus said that knowing God's truth and living it "will make you free."[8] Conversely, to be led and controlled by evil—such as drugs, alcohol, or other compulsive behaviors—is actually a form of slavery. We talk about how we become slaves to bad habits or addictions. We may even say, "The devil made me do it," as though we weren't really free, when we are really choosing to let the devil be in us.

But what about the kind of evil we neither seek nor choose, such as accidents, disease, and misfortune? Because we are not aware of any fault that brought such evil into our lives, we are easily disposed to cry out in protest: what did I do to deserve this? Instead, let us reflect on what God would want to be accomplished, so that the evil may be there for the reason it was permitted—that good might result. God's will is not to be seen in what happens to us, but in the opportunities that open themselves to us. We may have to know and experience some form of evil to overcome it, but that is part of the process of our spiritual growth.

Indeed, one of the uses of evil in our lives, in whatever measure, is that it provides a perspective to reflect on our lives and to choose to change. It is like the annual exercise of making New Year's resolutions, the observation of Lent, or the Jewish day of atonement on Yom Kippur. If we make a sincere effort to repent, we can rid ourselves of evil and become truly free.

Plato recognized in *The Republic* that we have to know evil—not necessarily from doing it but through observation and awareness—in order to reject evil and be free from it: "The judge should not be young. He should have learned to know evil, not from his own soul, but from late and long observation of the nature of evil in others: knowledge should be his guide, not personal experience."[9]

Part of what we observe, of course, which may chafe at our sense of justice and providence, is people all around us so who do not seem to be leading good, pious lives—indeed, perhaps the opposite—but who become wealthy, famous, and even idolized. And we do not see them openly punished by God.

But just as God's mercy falls on the just and unjust, we do not have to be devout to be successful in life. Material success can be a blessing or a curse, depending on whether it's a way to serve others or a platform for self-indulgence. Either way, the "success" of good or bad people can produce benefits for others. Whether people deemed successful in this life wind up in heaven or hell depends on their own motives and choices.

Consider the words of the psalmist: "I was envious of the arrogant; I saw the prosperity of the wicked . . . until I went into the sanctuary of God; then I perceived their end."[10]

We are certainly not alone in our struggles and temptations. Everyone is on the same journey. Indeed, the ancient journey of the children of Israel, fleeing from slavery in Egypt and wandering through the trials of the wilderness until being delivered into the Promised Land, still resonates in our own lives. That is because so much of living lies in the challenges we all must face, and in how we respond to them and grow from them.

It would be nice to think we all could find a blissful happiness without any hardships or challenges. For some people, it may be a dream of winning the lottery so they don't have to work anymore and can just "be happy." It doesn't work that way, and there have been plenty of examples of people winning fortunes who became quite miserable. We form our character through the way we respond to the situations and obstacles that test us in life.

The children of Israel suffered all sorts of setbacks and temptations on their journey and often wanted to quit. Temptation wrestling with our base, self-centered instincts and inclinations—is an essential part of our journey. This is the way we regenerate or are "born again," putting off our old life and letting a heavenly life take its place.

Our spiritual paths are unique to each of us. But the more we realize that we are all on similar journeys and help each other, and the more we let God lead us, the easier and more rewarding the journey can become.

We just need to be assured that challenges arise in life not to discourage us but to help us grow. Consider Mother Teresa: a saint of a person, whatever your faith, who put service to the most destitute of people above her own comfort. But even hers was not a life of bliss or even unswerving faith. We know that she often felt alone, enduring apparent silence and darkness from God. In the midst of her devotion she was tormented at times by doubt. But she kept on serving the desolate souls of Calcutta because she saw that work as the will of God. That gave her life meaning and kept bringing her closer to God.

We're not likely to face the squalor and deprivation that she chose to serve, but it can be easy at times to feel, as she did, that God isn't listening to our prayers or paying attention to our needs. As we fight the struggles between good and evil, between light and darkness in our lives, doubt about God's presence and mercy is part of the process of temptation and growth. If even Mother Teresa was able to harness her suffering and doubt and keep persevering to spread her little light and goodness in the world, can't we find a way in our own lives to do what God wants us to do, and not what our selfish inclinations tempt us to do?

"Deliver us from evil." God can do that for us. He is always working to deliver us from the wilderness of our lives into the promised land of heaven, where there is eternal deliverance from evil.

That's what God's coming on earth is all about: the "good tidings of great joy" with his Christmas birth, the temptations he endured, his eventual crucifixion, and the ultimate triumph of his resurrection at Easter. Swedenborg tells us that the Lord came on earth as Jesus Christ to put down the hells, which were threatening to overcome the world. There is still evil in the world, but it is in balance now. We still are free to choose it, but we truly can be "delivered from evil" with the hope and promise of eternal salvation.

"I have said this to you, so that in me you may have peace. In the world you face persecution. But take courage; I have conquered the world!"[11]

Suffering: The Crossroads of Faith

For sufferance is the badge of all our tribe.
>—William Shakespeare, *The Merchant of Venice*

Joy is not the absence of suffering. Joy is the presence of God.
>—Anonymous

The most authentic thing about us is our capacity to create, to overcome, to endure, to transform, to love and to be greater than our suffering.
>—Ben Okri

MOTHERS, PHILOSOPHERS, nurses, and theologians all have looked into the eyes of innocent, suffering children with the same anguished question: how could a good and loving God allow this to happen?

It's a question that has haunted theology from Job to the Holocaust, from personal family tragedies to sweeping catastrophes.

It is a theme coursing through the history of art and literature, poetry and drama.

Serious thinkers like Sigmund Freud and C. S. Lewis have probed the mysteries of suffering and come up wanting. Only Emanuel Swedenborg offers real, spiritual answers. They are effective because they came to him during years of revelation from God, not from human logic and speculation.

Let's look at this fundamental issue of "undeserved suffering" through the eyes of others, then consider the more satisfying answers that Swedenborg provides.

Rabbi Kushner begins his best-selling book by boldly asserting that "why bad things happen to good people" is "the only question that really matters."[1]

Why? Because that question is at the very heart of faith. Those who believe in God may be willing to accept some mysteries, but they want their faith to make sense. Belief in a loving, all-powerful God is hard to reconcile with all the apparently unfair suffering in the world. Those two things taken together just don't make sense—at least, not on the surface.

Rabbi Kushner says that virtually every meaningful conversation he's had with people about religion revolves around this issue. There just seems to be something fundamentally unjust about "the wrong people" getting sick, being hurt, or dying young.

As a rabbi, witnessing the daily toll of tragedy, he had to ask himself if he could continue to teach "that the world is good, and that a kind and loving God is responsible for what happens in it."[2]

One way many people have dealt with the paradox is to assume that we get what we deserve—as though suffering is some kind of divine punishment meted out for our sins. But what has an innocent baby done to "deserve" being born with a disease or deformity? Where is the justice in a promising student being killed in a car crash or a young mother dying of cancer?

As a parent of a child born with a horrible, incurable disease, a child who died in his early teens, Rabbi Kushner rejects the notion that somehow God chose him and his wife as "special" enough to handle such a challenge. And he rejects the idea that bad things happen to good people because it gives them what they deserve as punishment for past sins. That kind of thinking creates guilt where none belongs. It ascribes a quality to God that just does not fit, and can cause people to doubt God or even hate him.

The good rabbi finds comfort in the psalmist: "I lift up my eyes to the hills—from where will my help come? My help comes from the Lord, who made heaven and earth."[3]

Yes, it is help—love and healing—that comes from God, not the affliction. The universal hope, of course, is for another world beyond this life, where at last there is justice for all and everyone is healed and reunited. But the rabbi laments, "Neither

I nor any living person can know anything about the reality of that hope." [4]

In fact, Emanuel Swedenborg was permitted to report extensively on the reality of the spiritual world, on heaven and hell, and how the hope of a healing afterlife can be fulfilled for all. (See Swedenborg's *Heaven and Hell*, and this author's *Window to Eternity*, for vivid descriptions of the reality of life after death.)

Viktor Frankl, the Holocaust survivor, famously used hope and courage to transcend one of the most egregious examples of mass suffering in the history of the world. As a practicing psychiatrist, Frankl developed from his experience a treatment called logotherapy, a power-of-positive-thinking approach to crises and suffering. That theory—described in his well-known book *Man's Search for Meaning*—has given millions of people the tools for dealing more effectively with pain, grief, and suffering, if not all the answers.

Frankl said, "What man actually needs is not a tensionless state but rather the striving and struggling for some goal worthy of him. What he needs is not the discharge of tension at any cost, but the call of a potential meaning waiting to be fulfilled by him." [5]

That search for meaning is what led to his book, which is a wonderful manifestation of something good coming out of incredible evil.

In the depths of the despair of his Holocaust experience, Frankl came to realize that when everything else has been stripped away, people still have one last freedom that can never be taken from them: choosing their attitude. Obviously, the range of personal suffering we see in the world is extensive—and intensely personal—but being a victim of the abject hopelessness of the Holocaust may be the greatest extreme one can experience. In Auschwitz, Frankl found that the kind of prisoner one became was clearly the result of an inner decision. Those who considered themselves victims, without hope, quickly succumbed. Those who had a reason for living, who still found meaning in their lives, were the survivors.

Frankl cites a study at the Yale School of Medicine in which researchers were impressed by the number of prisoners of war in Vietnam "who explicitly claimed that although their captivity was extraordinarily stressful—filled with torture, disease, malnutrition, and solitary confinement—they nevertheless benefited from the experience, seeing it as a growth experience."[6]

Many experiences that we would not choose for ourselves actually provide just such opportunities for growth, for something good coming out of something bad. And like those prisoners in Vietnam, most of us seem to accept that whatever trials come into our lives are somehow essential in forming who we are.

We all know of people who rise above their suffering with a kind of nobility that makes them heroes, even if they don't see themselves that way. Some examples in public life:

> ❧ **Helen Keller**, the courageous woman born deaf, mute, and blind who overcame her disability with an uplifting spirit—and became a devoted reader of Swedenborg. "The world is full of suffering," she said. "It is also full of overcoming it."[7]

> ❧ **Lou Gehrig**, the "Iron Man" of the Babe Ruth-era New York Yankees, who contracted the terrible disease that now bears his name: ALS, amyotrophic lateral sclerosis. In one of the indelible moments in sports history, he bid farewell to his fans, his body ravaged by the disease, but his voice echoing through the Yankee Stadium loudspeakers: "Today, I consider myself the luckiest man on the face of the earth."

> ❧ **Morrie Schwartz**, immortalized by his devoted student Mitch Albom in the classic book *Tuesdays with*

Morrie. When Albom learned that his beloved old professor was dying of ALS, he began to visit him every Tuesday. The book became Morrie's final lesson and his lasting gift to the world: teaching us all how to live through the dignity of his own dying.

☙ **Jean-Dominique Bauby**, a French writer and editor who was paralyzed at age forty-three by a stroke that resulted in a condition called the "locked-in syndrome." He could not speak, eat, breathe on his own, or move a muscle except for his left eyelid. By blinking in code—more than two hundred thousand times—he dictated a popular book that has since become a movie, *The Diving Bell and the Butterfly.* Although his body was immobile, his spirit and imagination were free as a butterfly. That gave meaning to his life.

☙ **Erik Weihenmayer**, who lost his sight at age thirteen. He thought his life was over, but was inspired by Terry Fox, a brave man running across Canada on a prosthetic leg to raise money and awareness for cancer research. In Terry, Eric saw both intense agony and enormous triumph, and dedicated himself to rising above his own adversity—to incredible heights. He has climbed the seven tallest mountains in the world, worked with young blind people all over the world to give them a whole new way of seeing, and written two books that have helped transform lives: *Touch the Top of the World: A Blind Man's Journey to Climb Farther Than the Eye Can See* and *The Adversity Advantage: Turning Everyday Struggles into Everyday Greatness.*

All of these people had something in common—severe disabilities that most of us could not conceive of handling as well as they. No doubt they went through periods of doubt and despair about their "bad luck." But each made a decision that echoes every day among the bravest of sufferers.

They did not give in to self-pity. They did not wallow in questions of "Why me?" They did not let the cancers of cynicism, criticism, and complaining eat away at their spirit. They still found meaning in their lives—and added meaning to ours.

Ask a doctor about patients suffering from debilitating disease or injury, and he or she will likely put them into one of two categories: those who see themselves as victims and those who see themselves as survivors. The survivors make the best recovery. In Auschwitz, as Frankl observed, they were the ones who did survive.

C. S. Lewis, the English scholar and writer who gave us the classic Narnia series and some of the most profound books ever written on faith, also probed the mysteries of pain and suffering. Lewis called himself a "lapsed atheist," a man whose own common-sense questioning led him to become one of the great modern champions of Christianity.

The first of the books on his journey into faith was *The Problem of Pain*, written in 1940. It is a detached, philosophical look at the most fundamental of religious dilemmas. Twenty years later, his beloved wife, Joy Gresham, died of cancer just four years into their marriage. His book based on that experience, *A Grief Observed*, was intensely personal and from the heart.

The Problem of Pain contends that pain demands a better answer than what is on the surface. Lewis, still on his journey from atheism to confident faith, wrote: "If God were good, He would make His creatures perfectly happy, and if He were almighty He would be able to do what He wished. But the creatures are not happy. Therefore God lacks either goodness, or power, or both." Resolving the contradiction seemed "unanswerable."[8]

Lewis struggled to understand how anyone who made others suffer could have been created by God. He came to understand that it's all about God allowing for human freedom. Because we are free to make bad decisions as well as good ones, suffering is unfortunate but inevitable.

Our free will is God's best gift to us. However, we have the choice of either using that freedom nobly in serving others or abusing it and causing pain.

Sigmund Freud, another scholar with enormous influence, started from a similar place but came to very different conclusions. He, too, was greatly bothered by the theological and psychological implications of pain and suffering, and he wondered where God fit in.

Lewis progressed from atheism to faith, but the brilliant Freud was blind to spiritual answers. He was purely the scientist, trusting only what he could see—and what he saw didn't make sense. He did not believe true knowledge could come from revelation, although Swedenborg tells us it is the only way God can teach us about spiritual truth. Freud suffered throughout his life, emotionally and physically, and never accepted God because he couldn't resolve the question of suffering on a purely scientific basis.

Helen Keller, in her blindness, still was able to see what Swedenborg proclaims: God is always with us to help, even—and especially—in times of pain and suffering.

"Character cannot be developed in ease and quiet," she wrote. "Only through experience of trial and suffering can the soul be strengthened, vision cleared, ambition inspired and success achieved."[9]

Swedenborg also teaches that God does not *want* us to suffer just so that we can grow, as Lewis speculated. He *permits* us to suffer so that we *can* grow—with his help.

We may not be inclined to think much about God when things are going well. It is when times turn bad that suffering people rage, pray, and question God. We all know the wartime cliché about "no atheists in foxholes." But God is always in the foxholes and in the living rooms, in good times and bad, offering his love.

Perhaps the suffering of the innocent and helpless is hardest to reconcile. Nothing is more painful than to see a child victimized by a horrible disease or subject to criminal abuse. Jesus said to his disciples: "Let the little children come to me, and do not stop them; for it is to such as these that the kingdom of heaven belongs."[10] So why can it seem as though he isn't protecting all children from evil?

Again, it comes back to permission. Allowing everyone to be free means that people are also free to inflict pain and even death on others. But that does not mean God has stopped caring, or that he isn't in control. Innocent victims will know his love and his mercy to eternity.

When a biblical prophet complained bitterly about his misfortunes, we read that although God may have seemed to cause grief, "he will have compassion according to the abundance of his steadfast love; for he does not willingly afflict or grieve anyone."[11]

Suffering courses through history. There is even a sense that a person can't be a true artist without experiencing "noble suffering." In his classic drama *Agamemnon*, written in Greece in 458 BCE, Aeschylus claimed that "by suffering comes wisdom."

There are all kinds of suffering. Some of us seem to get more than our share, and others to get off lightly. But all of us have some trials and low points in life, and we may begin to appreciate how they help us to grow spiritually. We are meant to overcome the temptations we face and to repent of any pain we have caused others; if we are sincere in the process, our lives and our faith are strengthened. We may have to go through our own variations of Jesus's trials on Good Friday to get to the triumph of resurrection on Easter.

This is like the story of the merchant in Matthew 13 who sold all that he had to buy "the pearl of great price," which is likened to the kingdom of heaven. We know that a pearl is a precious jewel resulting from a grain of sand. The coarse sand irritates the oyster and the substance it secretes to overcome the pain becomes the pearl. So out of pain comes love, healing, and something precious and heavenly that was not there before.

Suffering always brings us to a crossroads of faith. The comfort in the teachings revealed through Swedenborg is that pain and suffering never come from God and are not willed by him. What he gives us are the tools to see how his providence works and to understand that it will always lead eventually to good.

Swedenborg does not address pain and suffering the way a psychologist would, in order to help us cope emotionally. Rather, he sees in our suffering various manifestations of evil as root causes—and as part of the process of overcoming evil in ourselves as we advance toward heaven.

Swedenborg does offer the soothing teaching that pain and suffering in the body are real but temporary conditions. "When we suffer physically, our soul does not suffer, it merely feels distress. After victory, God relieves that distress and washes it away like tears from our eyes." [12]

The "victory," of course, is the salvation that comes to us through a process of regeneration—suffering through temptations and then turning away from evil influences in our lives. And while we may have to endure some pain and suffering in our lives, Swedenborg assures us that in God's eyes everyone is born for heaven; [13] that he provides the means for everyone to be saved; [14] and that his "constant effort" is to conjoin us to himself and give us the happiness of heavenly life. [15]

There may also be some protection in pain and suffering, because Swedenborg also assures us that we cannot be reformed in states of disease, fear, misfortune, and altered mental states—

because we are not in freedom—but we are not judged in those states, either.[16]

So while we certainly may not wish for pain or suffering—for ourselves or anyone else—going through such trials may actually serve a good end by helping us to evaluate our lives and make better choices. God isn't in the pain and suffering, but he is always there to lead us to a higher state.

The bottom line in Swedenborg's teachings is that if evil had not come into the world through humanity's own choices—and our continuing bad choices—there would be no suffering. The injustice arises when innocent people suffer because of the choices or actions of others. But as we have seen, all pain and suffering—no matter how grievous—is permitted by God only so that his providence can lead eventually to good. In the midst of suffering we still can make choices: to rebel against the "injustice" of God or to reaffirm our faith in him and his guidance; to look for revenge or toward an attitude of charity and grace; to wallow in self-pity or look for ways to improve our lives and thinking. That is the freedom God wants us to feel and exercise.

As long as we only look at suffering—as Lewis and Freud did—we'll never really understand it. The mystery of human suffering is finally resolved in the teachings of Swedenborg so that we can see God's divine purpose; not in the suffering itself, but in the good end for which it is permitted.

So the question should not be: "Why me, God?" or "Why this innocent child?" but "What good end might be made possible through this suffering, and how can we cooperate with God in working toward that end?" That is where his purpose and his love are manifest.

Every day, every moment, people are suffering and asking the question: "Why, God?" And every day, every moment, God is reaching out to reverse that pain with his love. Whenever we reach the crossroads of pain and misfortune, we will know the way to follow him—through the "pearly gates" or "the pearl of great price" into his heavenly kingdom.

God will always be there. "They will hunger no more, and thirst no more . . . for the Lamb at the center of the throne will be their shepherd, and he will guide them to springs of the water of life, and God will wipe away every tear from their eyes."[17]

5

When Bad Things Happen
Disease, Disasters, Accidents, and War

For the son of man did not come to destroy men's lives, but to save them.

—Luke 9:56

Have we not come to such an impasse in the modern world that we must love our enemies—or else? The chain reaction of evil—hate begetting hate, wars producing more wars—must be broken, or else we shall be plunged into the abyss of annihilation.

—Martin Luther King Jr.

And almost everyone when age,
Disease, or sorrows strike him,
Inclines to think there is a God,
Or something very like Him.

—Arthur Hugh Clough

A BABY IS BORN with special needs that will impact his and his parents' whole lives. Every other baby born that day in the same hospital is normal.

A young mother succumbs to cancer and her friends and family are left with devastation. Why her? She doesn't deserve this.

Thousands of cars pass each other on a highway every day without incident—and in one instant, two cars collide and lives are forever changed.

Two young men in war are side by side in a bunker. One is killed by a grenade, the other is spared.

Is this all random? Just good and bad luck?

Are some people actually targeted by fate? Punished by God? Or just unlucky?

We have all heard about a man who just misses a flight that goes on to crash, and he is left to ponder: "Why was I spared?"

And what strange destiny put all those innocent victims on the planes that turned into bombs on September 11, or those in the twin towers of the World Trade Center on that fateful day?

It's so much bigger than Brother Juniper's search for answers among the five victims of the collapse of the Bridge of San Luis Rey. So where is God and his providence with all the innocent victims and suffering in diseases, accidents, natural disasters, and war?

Illness and Disease

When God created the world in the familiar Genesis story, the Garden of Eden was a beautiful, innocent place—heaven on earth. What defiled it was the free choice of Adam and Eve to eat of the forbidden Tree of Knowledge. That choice is what made them human, and the same freedom is what makes us human. God will never take that essential freedom away from us, because we would not be human without it.

For the sake of our freedom, we are suspended between the good sphere or influences of heaven and the opposite sphere or influences of hell. We are free at every moment to choose between them. Just as heaven is all around us—in the innocence of a baby, the beauty of nature, the joy of helping someone— so is the bad side of the world. It permeates our culture, from Internet pornography to road rage, from hatred to cruelty, from child abuse to murder, and even in things as simple as bad moods and hurtful comments. Bad things happen to good people because there are people in the world who do bad things at times. All of the consequences flowing from bad choices spread pain and misery throughout the world, and innocent people all too often are victims.

Swedenborg teaches that disease exists only because evil exists. It is not hard to imagine that heaven is in God's perfect order, where there is no evil and therefore no disease. It is the one place we can finally and absolutely be free of hell.

If we assume that somehow our own actions or choices bring on disease, how do we explain epidemics that afflict whole populations at the same time? What about children born with disease or stricken by it? They cannot have done or chosen anything evil that would cause their illness. And "visiting the iniquity of the parents"[1] on the child is impossible to reconcile with almost any concept of God.

Swedenborg assures us that illness or misfortune are not divine punishment but are side effects of people deliberately turning away from God. No one, no matter how good or inno-cent, is immune. Who gets a brain tumor may be just as random as who gets on a plane that crashes. None of this is God's will. But all of us can be helped by the good things in the world that *are* God's will, through the operation of his providence.

Disease still is subject to natural laws. A virus can affect an innocent person just because he or she got exposed to it, like being hit by a truck. What is ultimately comforting is that everything subject to natural laws—including disease—is also subject to the higher spiritual laws of divine providence.

In the parable of the blind man, when the disciples asked who had sinned to cause his blindness, Jesus said that neither the man nor his parents had sinned but that the man had been born blind "so that God's works might be revealed in him."[2] The Pharisees could not accept this miracle and challenged the man, who told them the simple, profound truth: "One thing I do know, that though I was blind, now I see."[3]

Few of us "see" so clearly the real impact of whatever hap-pens to us, but we may get a glimpse of God's power working in us through coping with and overcoming ordeals such as ill-ness. Because the good outcome of God's providence may not be realized until after death, that concept may be hard to accept on this natural plane. This is especially true when the disease is deadly and we see no triumph beyond the grace and dignity of the human spirit. But God working with us and in us, to heal us, is like the oyster developing a pearl out of our pain. As the psalmist put it: "It is good for me that I have been afflicted, that I might learn from your statutes."[4]

We need medical science to do all it can to eliminate the dis-eases that plague us. Cancer, for instance, is a good illustration of how the natural order of cells can be fatally corrupted, and we are desperate to find a cure to this "disorder." But we must work just as diligently to eliminate all the spiritual disorders in the world—lust, vengeance, cruelty, oppression—that incubate disease and misfortune.

No matter how successful we are at putting our spiritual lives in order, however, we all face the same end: death, and the passage into a new spiritual world.

If we could choose, no doubt we would want to pass away quietly and happily in our sleep, but few people seem to get out of this world easily. We see sad old people, shells of their former selves, lingering on in nursing homes with mind and body in decline. Sometimes there is prolonged suffering. Often there is frustration with ill health and not feeling useful.

So what do any of us do to "deserve" our fate? Swedenborg assures us that no matter what bad things may happen to us—even if we die prematurely or linger on in a diminished state—we are like that blind man who neither sinned nor is being punished for his parents' sin.

He writes: "The life of every person is foreseen by the Lord, as to how long he will live" and that from earliest infancy God's providence is watching over us "with a regard to a life to eternity."[5] He describes some of the factors that affect the length of our lives:

- How vital our use (or service to others) is in this world and how important it is to continue.

- The stage of our regeneration, which is the process of repenting from sin and learning to live by God's will rather than our own. This may work both ways: we die when we have gone as far as we can with regeneration in this life, or we die to save us for heaven before we might be irretrievably corrupted.

- The need for our use and service to others in the spiritual world and heaven. Swedenborg describes life in heaven as similar to our life on earth in many ways, with angels living in houses, holding jobs, and socializing with others. The difference is that in heaven, each person's work is what they love to do most of all, and if their service is needed in heaven, they may be called there "early."

As finite beings, we cannot know or judge these factors for ourselves or others, and it may never be clear at the time why any person dies or another lives. This is especially challenging when someone dies "before their time," because of illness, an accident, or war. What Swedenborg helps us to see is that humanity's evil is at the root of these misfortunes, but God's love is always leading to a better end. The more we can come to trust in God and his providence, the easier it can be to accept "untimely" death.

Almost everyone perceives that little children who die go to heaven. Many people are instinctively comforted that these children have been taken to "a better place." When someone ravaged by disease is dying, we like to think that with death he or she at least will finally be free from pain and suffering and will find peace. We also like to believe that the aged and infirm, who often have all kinds of physical and mental issues, will be made whole again and live normal, happy lives. That is because we have a perception—if not yet a confident faith—that God's kingdom is beyond all the trials of this world. Which is why Jesus said in his Sermon on the Mount: "Strive first for the kingdom of God and his righteousness, and all these things will be given to you."[6]

Accidents and Disasters

Swedenborg says very little directly about natural disasters: why a hurricane, an earthquake, or a tsunami can devastate a huge area and victimize thousands of people, for example, or why a bridge in San Luis Rey suddenly collapses, taking the lives of five people anonymous to the world.

What he does say is that there is a very close relationship between the spiritual and natural worlds, and that everything that happens in this world is directly linked to what is happening in the spiritual world, where all of God's creation actually begins. Consequently, something as seemingly random as a hurricane is a manifestation of turmoil between the forces of good and evil in the spiritual world. Swedenborg says wars in this world similarly reflect actual battles between good and bad spirits. The combatants in our earthly wars still are free to think and act on their own, of course, but what animates the lust for war and the zeal for peace is influenced on the spiritual plane.

Only heaven, in its perfect divine order, is completely free of the reach of evil. Swedenborg confirms the common assumption that heaven really is free of all the sorrows and pain that plague this world. The turmoil we see in this world springs from what Swedenborg calls the world of spirits—that intermediate realm between heaven and hell where everyone arrives after death and where the good and evil are eventually separated into heaven or hell.

This, at least—and at last—is much more satisfying than calling such disasters "acts of God." And it answers the popular assumption that somehow anything bad that happens to us is linked to "original sin," as though we are still being punished for the actions of Adam and Eve. Swedenborg writes extensively about hereditary inclinations to evil, explaining that they do not affect our spiritual state unless and until we consciously embrace them. And once a person freely chooses to make evil his own, he is actually choosing hell for himself.

In the Bible we read, "Are not five sparrows sold for two pennies? Yet not one of them is forgotten in God's sight. But even the hairs of your head are all counted. Do not be afraid; you are of more value than many sparrows."[7]

Swedenborg teaches consistently that God's providence is not only in the dramatic events that affect countless lives, but in every particular of every single person's life. As we saw in the story of the cataclysmic Lisbon earthquake and tsunami 250 years ago, that far-reaching devastation also seemed to lead to an incredible series of positive consequences throughout the world. And we all know personal stories where something good and unforeseen came out of a tragic circumstance.

Examples are all around us. They are the kind of illustration, in retrospect, of how good things really can come out of misfortune. Of course, some people may choose to see such happenings as pure coincidence, unrelated to any divine plan. But others see the hand of God—not interfering or manipulating, but with his love always triumphant.

We may try to explain away accidents and natural disasters as "acts of God," but they are never his will. In fact, often such events are caused by our own fallibilities. We create the cars and planes that sometimes crash, the ladders people fall from, the steps we slip on. Accidents often are the result of our own— or someone else's—bad choices and actions, such as speeding and driving recklessly. Some people build beautiful homes on beaches or hillsides, only to see them destroyed by hurricanes or mudslides that should have been anticipated. We even contribute to environmental disasters, such as dumping the toxic waste that may cause cancer in innocent victims. God is never in the accident—he neither causes nor stops it. He is in the aftermath, with his love always leading to healing and a happier outcome.

As for natural disasters, God created the "laws of nature." As with the laws of divine providence discussed earlier, he will not interfere with the laws of nature to suit our own idea of what is right. Indeed, the shifting of tectonic plates that results in an earthquake may be just such an example of the laws of nature at work—because God created the world to work that way, he will not change the natural course of events. And even in nature God restores balance and order, as we see most vividly with forest fires.

One of the most comforting teachings about accidents and disasters in Swedenborg's book *Heaven and Hell* is that people who die tragically later awaken in the other world to a sphere of love and peace, with no memory of fear, suffering, violence, pain, or terror. And those same people will be there when the time comes to welcome with joy those now mourning them in this world.

It is hard to see any benefit in the face of tragedy, but such experiences often do inspire us to reflect on our lives and reevaluate our priorities, which is one way of bending our lives toward good. It is also impossible to see all of the factors intertwined in any one event and to appreciate how intricately God's providence is working in each of our lives. Unraveling all of the repercussions of a tragedy—from a car crash to an earthquake affecting millions—is infinitely more complex than what Thornton Wilder tried to do with the five victims of *The Bridge of San Luis Rey* But in every thread of our lives there is God's awareness, love, and providence.

So rather than feeling sorry for ourselves in the face of misfortune, or railing against God as uncaring or unloving, we need to reflect on what we can do to help with what God wills, bringing something good out of misfortune.

Consider, for instance:

- Seeing and recognizing all that is harmful and evil in the world helps us to appreciate what is good—and to make good choices freely in our lives.

- Seeing others suffer helps us to be more sensitive and merciful, which spurs the progression from misfortune to good result.

- Tragedies can open ways for us to be useful to others. Witness the outpouring of service and kindness in the wake of September 11.

* Manifestations of selfishness, greed, and cruelty help us to recognize and work on our own failings, which is necessary for regeneration.

* Many times when people lose their homes in fires, hurricanes, or earthquakes, they reflect that these are only natural things of this world which can be replaced. Life and spiritual values suddenly have more meaning.

* Everyone wants to make a difference—to make the world a better place. We get plenty of motivation every day as we see the challenges.

* Finally, no matter how great or small the tragedy, whether it is a global or intensely personal experience, God is always there.

"Now there was a great wind, so strong it was splitting mountains and breaking rocks in pieces before the Lord, but the Lord was not in the wind; and after the wind an earthquake, but the Lord was not in the earthquake; and after the earthquake a fire; but the Lord was not in the fire; and after the fire a sound of sheer silence."[8]

War

You would think we would learn.

Throughout 3,500 years of recorded history, only 268 have been without war somewhere in the world. There is a sad futility to the concept that wars are decided by who kills the most of the other side, but we still don't seem to be able to stop.

There is always a cause worth dying for—and killing for. There have been "good wars" and "bad wars," necessary wars and inevitable wars, wars that changed history, wars of folly, and wars that are forgotten footnotes.

But why? What passions roil men to rally behind leaders and kill for a cause—for freedom, for power, for retribution, for greed—even to the extreme of brother against brother in civil wars?

Always there are voices saying, "Stop! There has to be a better way." And sometimes we can cool the emotions, restrain warmongers with diplomacy, or mount a strong enough defense to discourage others from attacking us. But among the baser instincts of men is a knee-jerk barbarism: settling disputes with anything from slurs and fists to guns and bombs.

Every war may be seen as a failure to reconcile differences, a hatred that first corrupts individual hearts and minds and then whole nations and armies. Some people leap to the cause. Some are dragged into it. Others have no choice; they are attacked.

World War I was so horrific and global that it was called "the war to end all wars." But the festering delusions and animosities of that war quickly sowed the seeds that erupted into World War II.

Now we look back at the horrors of that war and wonder. The Germans and Japanese then were the embodiment of evil in our eyes. Now they are among the free world's strongest allies and two of the most productive and stable nations of the world. Sons and grandsons of men who tried to kill each other now do business together. It is hard to imagine that we were such bitter enemies, that our people could be turned so hatefully against each other by the misguided nationalism exploited into a frenzy by Hirohito and Hitler.

That really was "the war to end all wars" because it was ended with two atomic bombs. In his epic novel *War and Remembrance*, Herman Wouk wrote: "If the hope is not the coming of the Prince of Peace, it has to be that in their hearts most people, even the most fanatical and boneheaded Marxists, even the craziest nationalists and revolutionaries, love their children and don't want to see them burn up. There is no politician imbecile enough, surely, to want a nuclear Leyte Gulf [a cataclysmic naval battle in World War II]. The future now seems to depend on that grim assumption. Either war is finished or we are."[9]

Well, war is not finished. The threat of nuclear Armageddon still hangs over the world. The instincts for battle have not changed, just the means.

Politics and situations change. America fought a bitter war for independence against England, and now these two countries are the strongest of allies. Sometimes people even forget why they were fighting, what made it all so important. And there is this sad perspective from an officer on the staff of General Thomas Jonathan "Stonewall" Jackson after Antietam—the bloodiest, costliest battle of the Civil War—who wrote: "The night after the battle was a fearful one. The dead and dying lay thick over the field as harvest sheaves. . . . Silent were the dead . . . and midnight hid all distinction between the blue and the gray."[10]

Isn't that telling? In the dark, no one could tell the difference between these men who saw nothing in the daylight but enemies who must be destroyed. But tragic as it was, the Civil War is what really put "united" in the United States of America. Now we all are a family again.

It was after the equally devastating Battle of Gettysburg that President Abraham Lincoln so eloquently summed up both the nobility and futility of war, and the mournful hope that attends all wars, in his Gettysburg Address: ". . . that these men shall not have died in vain."

The victims will not have died in vain only when we can address the spiritual as well as the earthly causes of war. For Swedenborg makes it clear that war, just like everything else in this world, has its roots in the spiritual world. The spiritual conflicts we all face—in temptations, in the daily battle of wills and temperaments—are just writ large in wars between nations.

We have seen throughout history that war brings out the best and the worst of the human spirit. We see incredible bravery, courage, commitment, love of country, and the ultimate in sacrifice for one's fellow human beings. We also see depraved brutality, cruelty, hatred, and wantonness. All of these attributes are manifestations of the spiritual combat at the root of all war: the eternal struggle of good versus evil, love of the world versus love of God, heaven against hell.

This is why Jesus, when he was sending out his disciples and warning them of the persecutions they would face in his name, said, "Do not think that I have come to bring peace on earth; I have not come to bring peace, but a sword." [11]

One reason why we are here on earth is to wield the sword of God's truth in our lives against the alluring power of the hells—to fight our own private wars.

Swedenborg teaches that wars of nations and peoples against each other are really larger manifestations of the same kind of underlying spiritual combat in the world of spirits.

He acknowledges that just because wars are permitted "in which so many people are killed and their wealth plundered," it is easy to doubt or deny any sense of divine providence operating in the world. But exactly because wars are "diametrically opposed to Christian caring," he says, they are not a part of God's providence but his permission. "If it were not for this permission, [God] could not lead us out of our evil, so we could not be reformed and saved. That is, unless evils were allowed to surface, we would not see them and therefore would not admit to them; so we could not be induced to resist them. That is why evils cannot be suppressed by some exercise of divine providence. If they were, they would stay closed in," like cancer, and "would spread and devour everything that is alive and human." [12]

When evil is not seen, acknowledged, and condemned, it festers. Think of Hitler's power to blind so many people to the evil he loosed upon the world and what a horrible war it took to bring his fanaticism under control.

Swedenborg says we all have something of that potential in us—not on such a grotesque scale, of course—but until we are saved we are like a "little hell," caught up in selfish tendencies and worldly pleasures. The process of salvation, he teaches, comes through the trials of temptation, which lead us to choose the way of repentance. We see these spiritual battles most nobly in the unimaginable temptations suffered by Jesus during his life on earth and just before his crucifixion. Early in his ministry, just after being baptized by John the Baptist, he was tempted by the devil:

"Again the devil took him to a very high mountain and showed him all the kingdoms of the world and their splendor; and he said to him, 'All these I will give you, if you will fall down and worship me.'"[13]

Swedenborg describes temptations, which we all experience in regeneration, as attacks from hell on the good things we love. Just as God is constantly lifting us toward heaven, the hells are fighting just as hard to drag us down. They do this by targeting what we love and care about most, creating doubt and anxiety in our own minds.

As Jesus was about to be crucified, he was attacked by the hells in all their fury. When he was condemned, the crowds "spat in his face and struck him," and taunted him, "Prophesy to us, you Messiah! Who is it that struck you?"[14] He was mocked with a crown of thorns as the "King of the Jews";[15] and "You who would destroy the temple and build it in three days, save yourself! If you are the Son of God, come down from the cross."[16]

This was the kind of "war" between heaven and hell we can scarcely imagine. But it was the essential culmination of what he came on earth to do—to conquer the hells, restore them to order, and give us the everlasting freedom to choose for ourselves between heaven and hell. This is why God "cannot rescue any of us from our hell unless we see that we are in it and want to be rescued. This cannot happen unless there are instances of permission that are caused by laws of divine providence."[17]

This is why, he continues, "there are lesser and greater wars." But whether greater or lesser, all are rooted in spiritual conflict that we aren't aware of; we just see the conflict in this world. This was as true for the wars described in the Bible, he says, as wars in his time—and presumably in ours.[18]

Good people and good nations do not want war. But it is a sad reality that evil people will do all in their power to control and subjugate others, and failing to take up arms against them can result in even greater loss of life and freedom. One reason why God permits war is so that its underlying evil can be seen and opposed, and we can work to turn evil toward good, just as God's providence does. As we see and fight against the evil in tyrants, we are summoned to look at ourselves and "remove the mote in our own eye." Just as appeasement of warmongers invites war, appeasing or justifying our own failings invites internal spiritual conflict. This is why we need to take up swords before we can have peace.

But whether the "war" is inside of us or played out on global battlefields, God and his providence are always there, guiding us to the way out.

Abraham Lincoln recognized this in the depth of his agony over the Civil War. In her masterful biography *Team of Rivals*, Doris Kearns Goodwin quotes Lincoln as saying: "If I had my way, this war would never have been commenced; if I had been allowed my way, this war would have ended before this, but we still find it continues; and we must believe that He permits it for some wise purpose of His own, mysterious and unknown to us; and though with our limited understanding we may not be able to comprehend it, yet we cannot but believe that He who made the world still governs it."[19]

"Blessed are the peacemakers," said Jesus in his Sermon on the Mount.[20] They are the ones who bring peace among nations, and they are the ones who bring peace within themselves by rooting out what stands against God and by choosing heaven.

That is why the ultimate prayer against the long, sad history of war is that we eventually reach the point that "they shall beat their swords into plowshares, and their spears into pruning hooks; nation shall not lift up sword against nation, neither shall they learn war any more."[21]

Wars on large, horrific scales may be prevented, and may have to be if Herman Wouk is right that "either war is finished or we are." But the "wars" within each of us, the spiritual fight against temptation, will continue because that is the divine purpose of life on earth—balancing between the influences of heaven and hell, and freedom to choose between them.

6

Trusting in Providence

Those of steadfast mind you keep in peace—in peace because they trust in you.

—Isaiah 26:3

The antidote to frustration is a calm faith, not in your own cleverness, or in hard toil, but in God's guidance.

—Norman Vincent Peale

He that takes truth for his guide, and duty for his end, may safely trust to God's providence to lead him aright.

—Blaise Pascal

Even beginning to grasp what divine providence is and how it works isn't going to end all questions and remove all doubt.

Believing firmly in God, in his enduring love and guidance, still may not be enough when tragedy suddenly becomes intensely personal. There will always be bad things happening to good people that rock our faith and leave us questioning, or even raging against, God.

But there is one thing we should be sure of: nothing bad that happens in this world is ever God's will. There is just no way he wants the people he loves to suffer. Remember, he never does things to us and is always working with us. But reconciling his love with what he permits for the sake of our freedom still is a test of personal faith.

Almost everyone has had an experience that may never completely lose its pain. Every day things happen that can evoke tears and questions. But think about the very worst of all tragedies ever to occur on this earth. For Christians, the darkest day of human history was the crucifixion of Jesus Christ. Wasn't that the ultimate example of God permitting what surely was not his will—the sacrifice of "his only begotten son"—for the sake of our freedom and happiness?

And isn't that still the ultimate example of providence, the way God is always there, in the aftermath, turning the eventual outcome toward good? Swedenborg clearly states that everyone born in the world has the opportunity to be saved and to choose an eternity in heaven only because of Christ's crucifixion and resurrection, his temptations, and his triumph over the hells that would enslave us.

This faith is the beginning of trust, trust in God's transcendent love and trust in the leading of his providence.

When we understand who God is and how he operates through divine providence in every particular of our lives, how can we not trust in him and be at peace?

As nineteenth-century English evangelist and philanthropist George Müller put it: "Where faith begins, anxiety ends; where anxiety begins, faith ends."[1]

Such faith—or trust in God—is not easily come by. It is too easy to trust first in ourselves, so confident that we could control the world more carefully than all the apparently random havoc we see. It is the height of arrogance to think that we could do a better job of managing the intricacies of everything that impacts our lives, plus all of the myriad unintended consequences. Consider: If God could control the world so that nothing bad could ever happen, would you really want to live without the freedom to make mistakes and learn from them? How else could you grow spiritually?

While we are asking ourselves why a loving God would permit evil and disorder in the world, we should also ask why he allows us to have evil in our own hearts. Because he loves us, he allows us to be free, even to violate that love with our bad choices. Consider that of all God's creatures, only humans can violate his order, and we are the sole cause of disorders in the world. Taking a good tool and trying to use it the wrong way won't work. Neither do our lives work properly when we choose to operate outside of God's order.

God does not manipulate the world to suit our whims. Rather, he works through his providence to change us for the better from the inside out.

As the novelist Henry Miller observed: "The world has not to be put in order: the world is order incarnate. It is for us to put ourselves in unison with this order."[2]

We are not supposed to be impassive philosophers pondering where God fits into our lives without doing anything about it. Just as Pearl Harbor and September 11 plunged the United States into global wars, we need to realize that we are caught up in a great war between heaven and hell. In war, unfortunately, there is collateral damage that victimizes innocent people. That type of ripple effect from evil is the fundamental reason, Swedenborg teaches, why bad things happen to good people.

Because of this ongoing war between good and evil, we are challenged to take up that sword of truth and become soldiers in the battle, not to be passive victims. This is what gives our lives purpose and meaning, and it is what should ultimately give us trust and hope.

We all face trials in life—pain, disappointment, maybe tragedy. Most of it we come to accept as part of learning and growing, part of life. The struggle is like the refiner's fire that removes impurities from metals in making precious jewelry.

It is when the trials become crushing, like the death of a child or the devastation of losing everything to a natural disaster, that it gets a lot harder to accept them as learning experiences. God does not choose to inflict such pain just to teach us lessons. But that is when a lot of hurting people understandably doubt God, and rail against him—or turn to him.

Swedenborg helps us to see such tragedies as manifestations of that spiritual battlefield, more like the fallout of an atomic bomb, with its indiscriminate victims, than one targeted bullet. Swedenborg assures us that as we join the fight against the hells that attack us, we also help many more people than just ourselves.

Does it seem unfair that we should all be caught up in this war, and its fallout, as part of choosing our own way? Consider the life of Jesus. Why couldn't he, of all people born on earth, just live a life of peace and contentment? Why, as soon as he was baptized by John the Baptist, did he have to endure forty days and forty nights of terrible temptation in the wilderness? Why did he have to suffer the ignominy and anguish of being put to death on a cross, before an angry mob, at just thirty-three years of age?

The answer, of course, is that he came into the world to fight for us. He had a clear mission: to overcome the hells for the sake of our freedom, for everyone then alive and for everyone ever to be born in this world. He offered not just freedom *from*, but freedom *for*—the opportunity to elevate our lives. Indeed, he came down among us so that each of us could have the hope of becoming a better person and ultimately an angel in his heaven.

While he did this for all humanity, he did it very personally for each one of us. And so we have a similar mission in life: to fight against temptations, to endure pain if it takes pain, and to regenerate, that is, to become "born again" by freeing ourselves from evil desires or inclinations in our lives.

This why the story of the children of Israel—freed from slavery in Egypt only to wander for forty years in the wilderness before being delivered in the Promised Land—is a metaphor for the wandering, searching, trials, and sometimes desolation in our own lives. This journey calls on us to free ourselves from slavery to our desires and determine to live more spiritually. And this battle, with the inspiration of Jesus's life, has to be our purpose in life if our victory, like God's victory over the hells and an eternity of peace in heaven, is to be achieved.

We may feel at any point that we are doing fine on our own with our lives, but the more we trust in God, the more enduring our victories will be. Getting to such a level of trust is not easy. Some people tend to see God as remote and even vengeful. They may see his providence as a capricious thing—that he can be angry, that he punishes people, that he can be swayed by prayer. Swedenborg teaches just the opposite: that he is a God of pure love, always present with us, and always there to lift and save us, if we will but follow.

In Swedenborg's writings, divine providence is a profound and complex doctrine, but simple and basic in its concepts. For centuries, theologians have been studying, pondering, and debating the way God leads us. But even a child can grasp the premise that he loves each of us and has a plan for our lives.

Within the teachings given through Swedenborg, we find complete trust in God and the way he leads. We see him in all his mercy, feel and understand his love, and begin to comprehend the spiritual plane, where life has its real meaning.

While God is doing all he can continually to lead and raise us up to heaven, he leaves us free to choose differently. And it should be obvious that if we deliberately put ourselves outside of heaven by the choices we make, and "make our bed in hell," we should not expect to enjoy heaven's blessings.

Choosing to trust in God's leading by living according to his commandments and loving one another is to immerse yourself, in Swedenborg's words, in the "stream of providence." Trusting in him is like a current running through your life and leading to a good end, no matter what whirlpools and rapids and eddies come up along the way. That trust also means realizing that when we turn our backs on God, it is as though we are swimming upstream, with all the frustration that entails.

What holds us back from taking the plunge into trusting in this stream of providence? A lot of hesitancy lies in doubt—just not knowing or understanding enough to trust completely in providence. It is easy to doubt when, for instance, we see evil people exalted or prospering. But providence lies in looking to spiritual ends, not worldly life.

We may see others deny God and any idea of providence outright, which is also a free choice protected by God. It is easy to be fatalistic about life, to believe that there is little or nothing we can do to change our circumstances, and this may lead to indifference about God. But the biggest obstacle to trust is simply worry.

Fear and worry are the opposites of trust, and they lead away from God. That is why Jesus taught the lesson in his Sermon on the Mount, "do not worry about your life, what you will eat or what you will drink, or . . . what you will wear."[3]

"Not worrying about your life" refers not just to people who are concerned about the future, but to those who trust only in themselves instead of God. People who focus just on the things of the world often are not content with their lot.

People who trust in God's leading, on the other hand, still plan for the future, but they aren't burdened with anxiety. They are content with their lot and unruffled by whatever life brings them. They are in harmony with the psalmist: "Let your steadfast love, O Lord, be upon us, even as we hope in you."[4]

Whether or not we feel that confident trust, Swedenborg assures us that those who place themselves in the "stream of providence" are carried along continually to true happiness, no matter what the appearance may be to the contrary at any one time. As Swedenborg puts it: "There is a kind of field that constantly emanates from the Lord, which pulls all toward heaven. It fills the entire spiritual world and the entire physical world. It is like a strong current in the ocean that secretly carries ships along."[5]

Many books have been written and theories expounded on the "secret of happiness." There is no secret in Swedenborg's writings. The explanation is simple: Real happiness comes only in states of peace, which result from complete trust in God. Those who trust only in their own instincts and close themselves off from the power of God's love limit the happiness that God yearns to give them.

But there is hope for everyone. God does not favor only the people who are trying to live a good life according to his commandments. His love is constant and unconditional, raining "on the righteous and unrighteous."[6]

The difference in the way God's love is projected and received is not with him but within each of us. We choose whether to go with the flow of the stream of providence or to seek our own way. God said: "Listen! I am standing at the door, knocking; if you hear my voice and open the door, I will come in to you and eat with you, and you with me."[7] He does not knock randomly or selectively. He knocks for any and all who will answer.

Trust in providence is not meant to be passive. It demands of us that we acknowledge what God wants for us and from us, and accept where he is leading us.

Trusting in God actually frees us from the influence of the hells, which are always looking for ways to exploit our anxieties and vulnerabilities, our doubts and frustrations, and any morbid feelings that life is meaningless.

Prayer is the way many of us ask God for help in our lives, but there are all kinds of prayer. He does not respond to prayers that would take away freedom: "Lord, get me out of this mess" or "Please stop this war." He responds to prayers which demonstrate that we are ready to work with him and to trust in him. This is when we are ready to incorporate his love and truth in all we do to try to make this a better world, to build peace from the inside out. This is the prayer: "Your kingdom come. Your will be done, on earth as it is in heaven."[8]

One of the best examples of trust in the Bible is the story of Joseph, who was sold into slavery in Egypt by his brothers. They were surprisingly reunited when the brothers came seeking relief from famine. The brothers were understandably afraid of what Joseph, in his elevated position as advisor to the Pharaoh, would do to get back at them. But Joseph was forgiving, because he understood how God leads through his providence, saying to his brothers: "Even though you intended to do harm to me, God intended it for good, in order to preserve a numerous people, as he is doing today."[9]

God wants us not only to be trusting, but to be optimistic.

Helen Keller, a devoted reader of Swedenborg, said: "No pessimist ever discovered the secret of the stars, or sailed to an uncharted land, or opened a new heaven to the human spirit."[10]

Consider the prophet Elisha, surrounded by a hostile army of Syrians, whose servant said to him: "Alas, master! What shall we do?" And Elisha answered, "Do not be afraid, for there are more with us than there are with them." And when Elisha prayed that his servant could see what he meant, "The Lord opened the eyes of the servant; and he saw; the mountain was full of horses and chariots of fire all around Elisha."[11]

God is giving us a picture here of our own lives, when we see all of the obstacles arrayed against us and all that we have to fight against. He does not want us to feel overwhelmed, but rather optimistic that by trusting in him we, too, come to see "that there are more with us than there are with them."

Another mental picture given by Swedenborg is that your life is like a tree that cannot grow of its own will but springs from the seed created by God and bears fruit only with his nurturing.[12] Similarly, you were created by God to grow into an angel by choosing—in this life and the next—to live as an angel. That means loving God, living his commandments, serving the neighbor. This cannot be done completely by yourself. God is helping and guiding all along the way, providing more power than all that may seem to be against you. You can chop down a tree, or let it wither and die without water, and you can choose to turn away from God's leading in your life. But he will never stop trying to lift you up to be an angel.

Viktor Frankl knew about both the power of optimism and the doom of pessimism. In the prison camps of the Holocaust, he found that those who saw no meaning in their lives—who felt they had nothing to live for—just gave up and died. We see the echoes in today's culture with those who see no future for themselves, who feel life is meaningless, and try to escape into drugs or alcohol. People can have enough to live by, but not enough to live for. They may have means, but not meaning, which can lead to depression, aggression, addiction, dropping out, and giving up.

Frankl said that those prisoners of war in Vietnam who suffered so terribly, but still felt the experience was an important part of their lives, lived the reality of finding something good—a more meaningful perspective of life—coming out of something bad. He calls this "the defiant power of the human spirit."

Shakespeare knew something of this feeling—the way adversity in our lives can lead to good:

> Sweet are the uses of adversity;
> Which, like the toad, ugly and venomous,
> Wears yet a precious jewel in his head;
> And this our life, exempt from public haunt.
> Finds tongues in trees, books in running brooks,
> Sermons in stone, and good in everything. [13]

The feeling of meaninglessness also can come from not feeling useful, and elderly people are especially susceptible to this. Someone who has grown feeble and dependent in old age begins to feel useless and may begin to doubt that God still cares. But a lot of people's usefulness lies in their ability to exert a good influence on other people, and the dignity, character, and wisdom of the elderly continue to make them valuable members of society.

Still, the search for meaning in our lives may be elusive, whatever our age or circumstances. It seems to make sense that everything that happens to us, good and bad, should have meaning and purpose, if only we could discover God's plan.

We incline to the tenets of our faith, but often do not find satisfactory answers. Indeed, we may be tempted to ask why there are so many religions in the world, each with its own confident claims, instead of God simply providing one true religion for all. But this may be the ultimate example of God leaving us in freedom. Most religions have common beliefs: something like the Ten Commandments, and requirements to love both the divine and one's neighbors. Swedenborg clearly teaches that anyone and everyone can be saved and taken into heaven if he or she acknowledges God and lives a good and useful life of faith and conscience.

That does not mean living an ascetic life, removed from the world, but living a life fully engaged in the world, being informed, aware, involved, and useful. We see people born into privilege who waste their lives and end up miserable, and we see people born into trying circumstances who rise to achieve success and happiness. Everyone, no matter what the circumstances of his or her birth, can choose to be useful.

This is one of the comforts of what has been revealed to Swedenborg—that everyone is born for heaven, and that God loves each one of us and never stops trying to elevate us to heaven. We may see a world filled with ugliness and people doing bad things to good people, but Swedenborg wants us to know that heaven is being filled every day with good people.

Trusting in God's care is not easy, especially in trying times. But as we ask God for peace, trust will grow. And the more we are able to trust in him, the more peace we will feel in our lives.

There will be questions and doubts, no matter how strong and confident our faith. But understanding what divine providence is—how it works for our eternal salvation, and how God's love and guidance always triumph if we let them—should nurture a calm sense that even if we don't understand why bad things happen, we can still try to trust in God.

Swedenborg writes: "Peace holds within itself trust in the Lord, the trust that he governs all things and provides all things, that he leads toward an end that is good. When we believe these things about him we are at peace, since we fear nothing and no anxiety about things to come disturbs us. How far we attain this state depends on how far we come to love the Lord."[14]

And then we have this ultimate promise from God:

> Come unto me, all you that are weary and
>   carrying heavy burdens,
> and I will give you rest.
> Take my yoke upon you, and learn from me;
> for I am gentle and humble in heart,
> and you will find rest for your souls.
> For my yoke is easy, and my burden is light.[15]

Notes

Introduction

1. C. S. Lewis, *A Grief Observed* (New York: The Seabury Press, 1961), 7.
2. Ibid.
3. Helen Keller, *My Religion* (New York: Swedenborg Foundation, 1953), 17, 25.
4. R.W. Emerson, *Representative Men* (Boston: Houghton Mifflin, 1930), 102–103.
5. Frederick G. Kenyon, ed., *The Letters of Elizabeth Barrett Browning* (New York: Macmillan, 1898), 34.
6. Ps. 139:6.

Chapter 1

1. Gen. 28:15.
2. Gen. 50:20.
3. John 9:2–3.
4. Emanuel Swedenborg, *Secrets of Heaven*, vol. 1, trans. Lisa Hyatt Cooper (West Chester, PA: Swedenborg Foundation, 2008), §245.
5. Harold S. Kushner, *When Bad Things Happen to Good People* (New York: Avon Books, 1983), 127.
6. Job 1:1.
7. Job 7:20–21.
8. Job 42:10.

9. Viktor E. Frankl, *Man's Search for Meaning* (New York: Simon & Schuster, 1984), 96.

10. Ibid., 9.

11. Thornton Wilder, *The Bridge of San Luis Rey* (New York: Time, 1963), 5.

12. Ibid., 139.

13. Kushner, *When Bad Things Happen to Good People*, 17.

14. Ibid., 18.

15. Matt. 5:45.

16. Job 38:2, 4.

17. *Eternity Magazine*, February 1978.

18. Emanuel Swedenborg, *Secrets of Heaven*, §8455; trans. Lisa Hyatt Cooper.

19. Gwen Florio and Terence Samuel, "En Route to Work, Vacation a Sudden Tragedy," *Philadelphia Inquirer*, October 20, 1996, sec. A.

Chapter 2

1. Michio Kaku, *Einstein's Cosmos* (New York: W. W. Norton & Co., 2005).

2. Emanuel Swedenborg, *Divine Providence*, trans. George F. Dole (West Chester, PA: Swedenborg Foundation, 2003), §§70–187.

3. Luke 12:29–31.

4. Luke 19:13–28 and Matt. 25:14–31.

5. Rev. 21:4.

Chapter 3

1. Num. 32:13.

2. Gen. 8:21.

3. Isa. 1:16.

4. Jean-Jacques Rousseau, *Emile, ou De l'Education*, Book 1 (1762).

5. Rev. 21:4.

6. John 3:3.
7. John 3:5.
8. John 8:32.
9. Plato, *The Republic* (New York: Tudor Publishing Co., 1936), 120.
10. Ps. 73:3, 17.
11. John 16:33.

Chapter 4

1. Kushner, *When Bad Things Happen to Good People*, 6.
2. Ibid., 7.
3. Ps. 121:1–2.
4. Kushner, *When Bad Things Happen to Good People*, 29.
5. Frankl, *Man's Search for Meaning*, 110.
6. Ibid., 147.
7. Helen Keller, *Helen Keller's Journal, 1936–1937* (New York, Doubleday, 1943), 17.
8. C. S. Lewis, *The Problem of Pain* (New York: Simon & Schuster, 1996), 23.
9. Keller, *Helen Keller's Journal, 1936–1937*, 34.
10. Matt. 19:14.
11. Lam. 3:32–33.
12. Emanuel Swedenborg, *True Christianity*, vol. 1, trans. Jonathan S. Rose (West Chester, PA: Swedenborg Foundation, 2006), §126.
13. Swedenborg, *Divine Providence*, §324:7.
14. Ibid., 325.
15. Ibid., 123:3.
16. Ibid., 142.
17. Rev. 7:16–17.

Chapter 5

1. Exod. 34:7.
2. John 9:3.

3. John 9:25.
4. Ps. 119:71.
5. Emanuel Swedenborg, *The Spiritual Diary* (London: Swedenborg Society, 1962), §5002.
6. Matt. 6:33.
7. Luke 12:6–7. See also Matt. 10:29–31.
8. I Kings 19:11–12.
9. Herman Wouk, *War and Remembrance* (Boston: Little, Brown & Co., 1978), 1055.
10. John O. Casler, *Four Years in the Stonewall Brigade* (Columbia, SC: University of South Carolina Press, 2005), 17.
11. Matt. 10:34.
12. Swedenborg, *Divine Providence*, §251.
13. Matt. 4:8–9.
14. Matt. 26:67–68.
15. Matt. 27:29.
16. Matt. 27:40.
17. Swedenborg, *Divine Providence*, §251:2.
18. Ibid.
19. Doris Kearns Goodwin, *Team of Rivals* (New York: Simon & Schuster, 2005), 562.
20. Matt. 5:9.
21. Micah 4:3.

Chapter 6

1. Arthur T. Pierson, *George Müller of Bristol* (New York: Fleming H. Revel Co., 1899), 437.
2. Henry Miller, *The Henry Miller Reader* (New York: New Directions Publishing, 1969), 363.
3. Matt. 6:25.
4. Ps. 33:22.
5. Emanuel Swedenborg, *True Christianity*, §652:3; trans. Jonathan S. Rose.

6. Matt. 5:45.

7. Rev. 3:20.

8. Matt. 6:10.

9. Gen. 50:20.

10. Keller, *Helen Keller's Journal, 1936–1937.*

11. 2 Kings 6:15–17.

12. Swedenborg, *Divine Providence*, §160.

13. William Shakespeare, *As You Like It* (Act II, Scene 1, Line 12).

14. Swedenborg, *Secrets of Heaven*, §8455; trans. Lisa Hyatt Cooper.

15. Matt. 11:28–30.

Bibliography

Frankl, Viktor E. *Man's Search for Meaning*. New York: Simon & Schuster, 1984.

Keller, Helen. *Helen Keller's Journal, 1936–1937*. New York: Doubleday, 1943.

———. *My Religion*. New York: Swedenborg Foundation, 1953.

Kushner, Harold S. *When Bad Things Happen to Good People*. New York: Avon Books, 1983.

Lewis, C. S. *A Grief Observed*. New York: The Seabury Press, 1961.

———. *The Problem of Pain*. New York: Simon & Schuster, 1996.

Swedenborg, Emanuel. *Divine Providence*. Translated by George F. Dole. West Chester, PA: Swedenborg Foundation, 2003.

———. *Secrets of Heaven*. Translated by Lisa Hyatt Cooper. West Chester, PA: Swedenborg Foundation, 2008.

———. *The Spiritual Diary*. London: Swedenborg Society, 1962.

———. *True Christianity*. Translated by Jonathan S. Rose. West Chester, PA: Swedenborg Foundation, 2006.

Wilder, Thornton. *The Bridge of San Luis Rey*. New York: Time, 1963.